# TONI MORRISON
# EXPLAINED

# TONI MORRISON
# EXPLAINED

A Reader's
Road Map
to the
Novels

## RON DAVID

Random House
New York

*Toni Morrison Explained: A Reader's Road Map to the Novels*

Copyright © 2000 by Ron David

Excerpts used by permission of Toni Morrison.

Published in the United States by Random House, Inc., New York and simultaneously in Canada by Random House of Canada Limited.

This book is available for special purchases in bulk by organizations and institutions, not for resale, at special discounts. Please direct your inquiries to the Random House Special Sales Department, toll-free 888-591-1200 or fax 212-572-4961.

Please address inquiries about electronic licensing of reference products, for use on a network or in software or on CD-ROM, to the Subsidiary Rights Department, Random House Reference & Information Publishing, fax 212-940-7370.

Visit the Random House Reference & Information Publishing Web site at www.randomwords.com

Library of Congress Cataloging-in-Publication Data
David, Ron
    Toni Morrison explained: a reader's road map to the novels/Ron David.--1st ed.
      p. cm.
    Includes bibliographical references and index
    ISBN 0-375-70732-8
    1. Morrison, Toni—Criticism and interpretation. 2. Afro-American women in literature.
    3. Afro-Americans in literature. 4. Women and literature—United States—History—20th century. I. Title.
    PS3563.O8749 Z614 2000
    813'.54—dc21                                  00-022221
Typeset by Allentown Digital Services, a division of RR Donnelley & Sons
Typeset and printed in the United States of America

First edition
0  9  8  7  6  5  4  3  2  1
April 2000
ISBN 0-375-70732-8
SAP Network: 10038435

New York   Toronto   London   Sydney   Auckland

# CONTENTS

# AUTHOR'S NOTE

This book is so far from the average introduction to a famous author that I'd like to give you some idea of what you're in for.

It is what it is for only one reason: I have never seen the kind of intro to an author that I would love to read, so I've tried to write one myself.

**WARNING: This book may be hazardous to your literary pretensions.**

If you want to read this book in the spirit in which I wrote it, put quote marks around the word "explained" in the title. Good. Now we've made the word ironic. Now it says, "If you think I'm going to claim that I can explain Toni Morrison, forget it!—My mama didn't raise any kids that dumb!" Reason #1: I've challenged, confronted, and told the plain truth (my version, not God's) to Toni Morrison's fans, fanatics, critics, and Toni Morrison herself; I'm not going to shoot myself in the head by claiming to explain her. Reason #2: The word "explain" implies that there is an answer and that I will give you that answer. There isn't and I can't. How do I explain why it's an affront to the truth to even claim to explain a great novel? The truest answer comes from Morrison herself. *Paradise,* TM's spectacularly misunderstood novel, leans heavily on the Gnostic Gospels, an early version of Christianity that rejected the notion that anyone could explain God or Christ or the religious experience to you or for you. It is a spiritual experience that can only be known directly, one-on-one. I see God in one way, you may see God as a Woman or a Spirit or a Lion With Wings.

A great novel is not a list of facts that someone can explain to you. A great novel is an experience, aesthetic or spiritual (or both), that can only be known directly, one-on-one. You see a novel in one way, I see it in another; it changes you and you change it. I don't want you to see Toni Morrison's novels through my eyes.

I want to help you experience Morrison's novels directly, with nothing between you and them.

I'm going to tell you something I am sure you've never heard: You don't need a college degree. You don't need special training. You don't have to be a certain age or any other thing. No matter what your age or education is, you, EXACTLY as you are NOW, have everything you need to read any book you're curious about. IF you have the guts to try. If you make mistakes or feel foolish, well, some of the most important lessons in this book are the times when I was wrong or ignorant or made a fool of myself. I left them in the book so you'll know you aren't alone. (And wait'll I tell you how the best critics in the country flubbed TM's novel *Paradise*.)

**Q:** *Can you give some sense of what your book is like?*

This book is not written in the pedantic doubletalk of "real" Literary Criticism. It's as far from that pretentious Professorspeak as I could make it. I think the odds are about twenty-to-one that you'll like my Fake Lit Crit a whole lot better than the Real Thing (I think you'll learn more, too), but I'm not competing with other styles of Lit Crit. As I said, I tried to write the kind of intro to an author that I would love to read: creative, provocative, irreverent, passionate, funny, spontaneous, and real. My approach will strike some people as radical and outrageous, but speaking plain English was the only way I could come close to achieving the almost impossible the goals I set for this book.

**Q:** *What are your goals—or your book's goals?*

▪ I tried to write a book that would compel you to read Toni Morrison's novels.

▪ I tried to provoke critics, reviewers, and Morrison fans to rethink TM's novels by accusing them of being led by the nose by Morrison's interpretations of her own novels. I offered different interpretations of her novels. (I'm sure they'll thank me.)

▪ Above all, I tried to write a book that would give anyone, regardless of age or education, everything they needed to understand and enjoy Toni Morrison's novels. The only requirement was the ability to read. (I knew adults with college degrees who didn't understand Morrison's novels and I wanted to write a book that would enlighten anyone, from 14-year-old street kids to your great-grandmother. What is this fool smokin'?)

**Q:** *Is it possible to write a book that speaks to very naive readers and experts alike?*

Let's pretend that it's possible and try to figure out how to do it. Traditional literary criticism is certainly not the answer. Most people consider it so boring and pretentious that, instead of attracting people to books, it repels them. I couldn't find a book that came near what I wanted—Lit Crit that people actually enjoyed!—but I realized that what seemed impossible in books happens so effortlessly and naturally when people talk to each other that you don't even notice it. My friends and I talk about books in the same way, and in the same language, that we talk about everything else. When I discuss books with the teenagers who smoke me in basketball, I don't change, they don't change. What can they understand?—anything they're interested in. Just be my same middle-aged Detroit street kid self. I've already written three books in my Always Be Yourself language. Not only will it speak to anybody, but it feels so natural. Morrison believes that novels should be written in "spoken" language. I believe that everything, including literary criticism, should be written in spoken language. You and I, hanging out over coffee, talking like real people. Our ideas are as subtle and complex as the Old Lit Critters, but we are grounded by the beautiful concept that I stole from (British poet/critic) I. A. Richards—if you speak in plain language, you can't con your readers (or yourself) into thinking that you've come up with a new idea when all you have is a new word.

**Q:** *How do you plan to teach Toni Morrison to the most naive readers?*

By doing one thing on the surface and another thing underneath. On the surface, we'll check out the principles and goals that underlie Morrison's work, like her intention to elbow the Eurocentric novel aside to make room for other kinds of novels. And we'll get a clear understanding of what TM calls the African-American novel. We'll examine the eleven characteristics that Morrison calls African-American and track them from book to book to see how close she's coming. As we move along, we'll try to understand what novelists do and how novels work. I'll give you some hints of what to look for in TM's novels, then we'll go through the novels one at a time. For each novel, I'll give you all the conventional elements (plots, characters, themes, etc.) and I'll try to give you some idea of how Morrison interweaves past/present, inner/outer reality, individual/ancestral consciousness, and the myths/legends of Africa and its diaspora in language so beautiful it stops your breath. I'll also give you a good sample of what the critics say about each novel, and we'll check out TM's comments on the work. I'll give you the conventional interpretation of each novel, then I will do what I ask you to do: come up with your own interpretation of the novel that is as plausible as you can make it. If plausible isn't working for you, make it as pleasurable as you can. What we're shooting for isn't Literary Criticism, it's Literary Hedonism: the pursuit of sheer pleasure through books. That's on the surface.

This is underneath: the one ingredient that a teacher needs most isn't information, it's enthusiasm. If the teacher is fired up about his subject, the student overheats too. Add the observation that They can learn anything they're interested in, and you can apply it to anybody of any age or education. No matter how much information I give you, it will be nothing compared to the information you'll get if we get you fired up enough to seek out your own information. What are the most important qualities a student can bring to the table? Probably curiosity and stick-to-it-iveness. If you don't quit, you get it. So no matter what I'm saying on the surface, the Big Stuff is underneath: trying to excite you, pique your curiosity, prod you into doing some research on your own, but above all, I try to con you into having some confidence. Everything you need to read Toni Morrison—or Faulkner or Shakespeare—is already there. All we have to do is get you to believe it. Although we'll bend over backwards to respect the author's goals, we won't allow them to control our opinion of her work. Which brings us to a couple of the other things that give this book an identity all its own: its complete honesty and its sense of humor.

**HONESTY:** If you aren't ready for a completely honest book on Toni Morrison, you don't want to read this book. I take that back—you NEED this book. If there are times when I seem too rough, consider this: The harsher your criticism is, the more weight your compliments carry. I have been so put off by the fawning that passes for reviews, interviews, or articles about Toni Morrison that I have almost stopped reading Morrison's breathtakingly beautiful writing. (Dear Toni Morrison fans: Stop protecting her. You'll attract more people to her books if you drop the unrelieved gushing.)

**HUMOR:** Toni Morrison is in grave danger of being treated like a sacred cow. I have done my best to protect her from that cruel fate. Honesty and humor help us bring readers to Toni Morrison in another way: As soon any reader with half a brain senses that a critic or reviewer is sucking up to the author he's writing about, he loses all credibility.

**Q:** *Does this book focus on a particular novel or is it spread evenly among the herd?*

The book's focal point is *Paradise,* Morrison's only novel since her Nobel Prize. *Paradise* may (or may not) be the hottest literary novel of all time: THREE reviews in the *New York Times*; a seven-page cover story in *Time*; a five-page review in the *New Yorker*—within two weeks of its publication, *Paradise* was given queen-sized reviews in virtually every newspaper and weekly in the country. But do you know what really kills me about *Paradise?*—All the reviews were wrong.

I read over 20 reviews, including the *Times, New Yorker, Time,* and the other big dudes. To a man, the best critics in the country misread and misunderstood Toni Morrison's novel as thoroughly as if they'd reviewed a new film of Othello without noticing that it was by the Three Stooges. And since they had missed the humor and irony, they took the book to mean almost the exact opposite of what it really did mean. Toni Morrison had played off of her Serious-as-a-Car-Wreck persona to make the critics read her reputation instead of her words. "Unbeknownst to us," the most serious woman in the world had turned into a Trickster Goddess, toying with us, jerking us around, planting "facts" that contradicted each other, and twins with photographic memories who had locking pneumonia and 140 ancestors—and they loved all 70 of them.

I agree, it is hard to believe, but once you read the chapter on *Paradise,* I don't think you'll have any doubts.

**Q:** *Is there anything you would have liked to put in this book but didn't—or couldn't?*

Yes. The intro to an author's work that I would love to read would give the author a chance to respond to the book. In plain English, that means that Toni Morrison's reactions would be part of this book. The author you're writing about should have the last word.

≈≈≈≈≈≈≈≈≈≈≈≈≈≈≈≈≈≈≈≈≈≈≈≈≈≈≈≈≈≈≈≈≈≈≈≈≈≈≈≈≈

To the reader:

Rather than load the text with detailed bibliographical information that would slow the book down and frighten away potential readers, we have taken the opposite approach. Within the text, you will find references to particular authors and works being cited. Additional bibliographic information can be found in the Bibliography, which begins on p. 195.

≈≈≈≈≈≈≈≈≈≈≈≈≈≈≈≈≈≈≈≈≈≈≈≈≈≈≈≈≈≈≈≈≈≈≈≈≈≈≈≈≈

# TONI MORRISON
# EXPLAINED

*Suddenly, like an elephant who has just found his anger and lifts his trunk over the heads of the little men who want his teeth or his hide or his flesh or his amazing strength, Pilate trumpeted for the sky itself to hear, "And she was loved."*
—Song of Solomon

# INTRODUCTION

After her divorce in 1964, Toni Morrison found herself in a situation that women everywhere can relate to: she had no husband; she had one child and another on the way; and she was jobless with no prospects for employment. So at the age of 33, Toni Morrison returned to her parents' home in Ohio. For many women, that could have been the beginning of the end; for Toni Morrison it was the beginning of a painful rebirth.

Twenty-nine years and six novels later, Toni Morrison won the Nobel Prize in literature. That meant, among other things, that her face would grace a Swedish postage stamp, she'd get $825,000 in spare change, and as of 1993, she would be considered the best fiction writer in the world. Not the best woman writer, not the best black writer or the best American writer—the best fiction writer in the world—period.

So if you haven't read Toni Morrison, this book will introduce you to her seven novels (plot descriptions, subtexts, reviews, Toni's comments on her own work) so that you can decide which of her books to read first. On the other hand, if you have read Toni Morrison, you may need this book even more. Although Morrison is a popular novelist who sells truckloads of books, much of the time, if we're honest about it, we aren't entirely sure what the literary Conjure Woman is talking about. And when we are sure, it turns out we are half wrong or have only got the tip of the iceberg instead of the whole beautiful, brutal, brooding thing.

So here is the book you need to get friendly with Toni Morrison. It's about the woman, her books, her mission, her wordmusic, and all that writing she does between the lines . . . what writers call the *subtext*. Morrison's books are like the ocean: the surface is beautiful but everything that gives them life is underneath.

She's the kind of writer who can change your life.

Toni Morrison is also the kind of human being who, by the way she has lived her own life, can inspire you to take charge of yours. She didn't even start writing until she was thirty-five, all the while holding down a full-time job and raising two children. Her first novel wasn't published until she was near forty; still, she managed to become the first black woman ever to win literature's highest award—the Nobel Prize. Not only did Morrison blossom into what critic John Leonard called "the best writer working in America today," she also became one of the most influential editors in America. Toni Morrison challenges us—all of us: men and women, people of every color—to begin living the lives we believe in.

The enormity of Morrison's talent raises a question that begs for an answer: as a writer, Toni Morrison is one of the most magical beings ever to grow out of the earth—but as a human being, she is so, so normal that you wonder how somebody that normal can have the power to move us so much?

Before you're finished asking it, the question answers itself: Morrison's power to move us, to involve us, is grounded in her very normalness, her so-much-like-us-ness. She has lived through the soul-shriveling experiences of an "ordinary" life, including divorce, depression, racism, single motherhood, and being broke and friendless in a strange town.

Who is this woman?

To see Toni Morrison as she sees herself, you have to understand that her life doesn't begin with her . . .

To Toni Morrison, her life begins with the lives of her ancestors—

. . . with West African griots telling magical stories to people who listen with their bodies and respond with their lives.

. . . with the "Sixty Million and more" men, women, and children killed in Africa or during the Middle Passage, to whom she dedicated her shattering novel *Beloved.*

. . . with the 15 million Africans who were "lucky" enough to make it all the way to America where they were enslaved.

. . . with her grandfather, John Solomon Willis, an ex-slave who had owned 88 acres of land in Alabama until some Southern gentlemen cheated him out of it.

. . . with her grandmother who left her home in the South with seven children and thirty dollars because she feared white sexual violence against her daughters.

. . . with her aunts, great-aunts, uncles—all of those and more—they are all her ancestors. Modern people talk about their ancestors as if they were an abstraction, a "concept." Toni Morrison's ancestors aren't a concept—they're real. And sooner or later, as she told Judith Wilson from *Essence* magazine, she's going to have to face them:

> Since it was possible for my mother, my grandmother and her mother to do what they did . . . snatching children and . . . running away from the South and living in . . . a big city trying to stay alive and keep those children when you can't even read the road signs. . . . I know I can't go to those women and say, "Well, you know, my life is so hard. . . ." They don't want to hear that! . . . I don't want to meet them people nowhere—ever!—and have them look at me and say, "What were you doing back there?"

Got your head around that? Good. Now we can move on to the normal stuff.

*If you study the culture and art of African-Americans,*
*you are not studying a regional or minor*
*culture. What you are studying is America.*
    —TONI MORRISON TO CHARLIE ROSE

# HER LIFE

. . . he was a little boy under five, and all he heard was that Emancipation was
coming. . . . Because he could feel the excitement, the fear, the apprehension
as well as the glee, he knew something important was happening. Emancipation is coming! Nobody explained it to him—and he thought it was some
terrible monster. And on the day when he knew it was coming he just went
and hid under the bed. [Laughs.] Oh, poor baby.

                            —Toni Morrison, remembering her grandfather,
                            to Charles Ruas

## CHLOE ANTHONY WOFFORD

On February 18, 1931, in the midst of the Great Depression, fifty years (give
or take a decade) before she became an overnight success, Toni Morrison was
born Chloe Anthony Wofford in the windy little steel-mill town of Lorain,
Ohio. Her father, George, was a shipyard welder from Georgia. Her mother,
Ramah Willis Wofford, came from Alabama, but after those white Southern
gentlemen cheated Ramah's father out of his property—all 88 acres—Mr. John
Solomon Willis decided he'd had enough of the South, thank you, and worked
his family north through Kentucky and on up into Ohio.

Morrison describes Ohio as a unique state as far as black people are concerned. It's like two different states. Southern Ohio, bordering on Kentucky, was a haven for the Ku Klux Klan, complete with cross burnings and racist violence. Northern Ohio, bordering on Canada, had been part of the Underground Railroad that helped slaves escape to freedom.

The Willis family ended up in Lorain, pretty much as far north as you can get in Ohio. Lorain was about twenty-five miles west of Cleveland and thirteen miles from Oberlin, a town whose history symbolized the best of Middle America—it had been an important stop on the Underground Railroad, and its famous university had admitted blacks and women before any other college in the country. Lorain was a small industrial town filled with European immigrants and Southern blacks who had come North seeking freedom, education, and work in the steel mills.

Chloe's father was a dignified, hard-working man who held down three jobs at once, even during the Depression. He grew up in Georgia amidst the lynchings of young black men. That left him with a serious lack of affection for white folks. "People assume that a racist is a white person that doesn't like black people," says Morrison, "but the term simply means a person who believes that his race is superior to another race. My father in that sense really felt that all black people were better than all white people because their position was a moral one." (Douglas Century, *Toni Morrison,* 1994)

George Wofford often told his children that there could never be any harmony between the races because white people were simply too damned dumb to overcome the bigotry they were taught as kids. The first act of violence between the races that Toni Morrison remembers is seeing her father throw a white man down the stairs. Badassed old George suspected that the guy may have been following Chloe and her sister, so he threw the gentleman down the stairs first and asked questions later!

Chloe's mother Ramah (a name picked at random from the Bible) felt that people who grew up in a racist society could eventually be changed by education. (But she wasn't going to hold her breath until that happened.) Ramah was not as pugnacious as her husband, but she was every bit as strong. She didn't fight the system, she just kind of ignored it. If she went to a movie theater that had a "special" section for the black people, she ignored it and sat wherever she wanted.

There were no black neighborhoods in Lorain. Through most of Chloe's childhood, the Woffords had a Greek family on one side and an Italian family on the other—which didn't exactly please her father. Old George, like a black Archie Bunker with a supercharged vocabulary, wasn't too crazy about "foreigners"—he not so warmly referred to them as the "detritus of Europe."

The fact that blacks weren't forced to live in separate neighborhoods didn't mean that Lorain was some fantasy American melting pot completely devoid of racism. Morrison, as usual, went right to the heart of the matter:

> I went to school with white children—they were my friends. There was no awe, no fear. Only later, when things got . . . sexual . . . did I see how clear the lines really were. But when I was in first grade nobody thought I was inferior. I was the only black in the class and the only child who could read!
>
> —to Jean Strouse

The fact that Chloe was a middle child (she had an older sister and two younger brothers) made her feel somewhat anonymous. Like many introverted children, she liked books. She read the masterpieces of European literature and loved the great Russian novelists Dostoevsky and Tolstoy, and the English writer Jane Austen: "Those books were not written for a little black girl in Lorain, Ohio, but they were so magnificently done that I got them anyway—they spoke directly to me out of their own specificity." (Strouse, *Newsweek*, Mar. 30, 1981)

Chloe's grandmother wrote her dreams in a book, then decoded the symbols with the help of another book so she'd know what to bet on when she played the numbers. Morrison remembers that her own dreams were so lucky that her grandmother won money betting on them; then her dreams went dry, so her practical grandmother looked elsewhere for luck.

Chloe never even thought of being a writer—she wanted to be a dancer. Storytelling was such a natural part of her life that it never occurred to her to make it into something fancy like a career. Her parents would spend hours telling the children terrifying ghost stories. In later interviews, Morrison makes a point of stressing the fact that her parents were comrades—they shared the storytelling just as they shared everything else. Throughout her childhood, without even knowing it, she absorbed the folktales, myths, and songs that had been an important part of Southern black culture for centuries. Her mother's family were all musicians—her grandfather was a violinist; her mother played piano in silent-movie theaters and sang everything from opera and jazz to blues and the pop tunes of the day as she went about her chores. One children's song her mother's family sang began with the words, "Green, the only son of Solomon." It was a song that Morrison would use as the turning point in one of her most powerful novels.

At Lorain High School, Chloe was an excellent student. Only one person in her entire family had attended college, and Chloe was determined to be the second. She applied to Howard University, one of the nation's most prestigious black colleges, and at the tender age of 17, Chloe Wofford left Lorain for college in Washington, D.C.

## HOWARD UNIVERSITY

Howard University, founded in 1867 by a herd of white clergymen, started out as a school for black preachers and evolved into one of the best colleges in the country—"the capstone of Negro education." Howard, which occupies 130 acres of Washington, D.C., was home to legendary educators like Alain Locke, the philosopher/critic who was the point man of the Harlem Renaissance in the 1920s, and Sterling A. Brown, the poet/professor who helped establish African-American literary criticism. Among the university's graduates were former Supreme Court Justice Thurgood Marshall, opera singer Jessye Norman, and actor Ossie Davis. About half of America's black doctors, engineers, and architects are Howard graduates.

It was at Howard that Chloe changed her name to Toni. Although she majored in English, Toni liked the university theatrical company, the Howard Players, best. Black literary consciousness was virtually nonexistent in the late 1940s, and even at a black college like Howard, great African-American writers like Langston Hughes and Zora Neale Hurston weren't even part of the curriculum. As a member of the Howard University Players, Toni toured the Deep South. The group performed before black audiences and had virtually no contact with white Southerners. Seeing what life was like for Southern blacks gave Toni a taste of the undiluted racism that her parents had endured. For the first time, she began to understand what her ancestors had gone through.

After graduation, Toni went to Cornell University for her master's degree in English. Her master's thesis (which foreshadowed not only the literary style of her writing, but her predilection for grim subject matter) was on the theme of suicide in the novels of William Faulkner and Virginia Woolf.

After Cornell, Toni went to Texas Southern University in Houston to teach English. Oddly enough, it was here that the unpredictable young woman first began to think about black culture in more than personal terms. She began to see it as a subject for formal study, as an academic discipline.

She returned to Howard University in 1957 as an English teacher and met several people who would go on to play key roles in the struggle for African-American equality: the radical young poet Amiri Baraka (then LeRoi Jones); Andrew Young, who would become mayor of Atlanta and U.S. ambassador to the UN; Stokely Carmichael, a smart and lively wisecracker, who seemed born to be a bit of an outlaw.

## MARRIAGE

While teaching at Howard, Toni Wofford met and fell in love with Harold Morrison, a young architect from Jamaica. They were married in 1958, and their first son, Harold Ford, was born in 1961. Toni Morrison continued to teach at Howard after the birth of her son, but she began to feel restless. She decided to join a small writers' group, not because she wanted to be a writer, but because she needed the company of interesting people.

Each member of the group had to bring in a story for discussion. One week, Toni ran out of old writings to bring, and knowing that she had to dash off something new, she remembered a conversation she'd had with another little black girl growing up in Ohio: the little girl said she had stopped believing in God because, after two years of praying for blue eyes, God still had not given them to her.

It was 1962, the early years of the civil rights movement, and Morrison realized that this episode from her childhood said something profound about the way black children were taught to think about their identities from a very early age. Morrison quickly wrote out the story of the little girl who prayed for blue eyes. She read the story to the writers' group. They seemed to like it.

She put it in a drawer and forgot about it.

In 1964, pregnant with her second child, Toni Morrison left her position in the English Department of Howard University and, with her husband and son, took a trip to Europe. By the time she returned from Europe, her marriage had "dissolved in smoke." Toni Morrison, who is so specific in her novels, is very unspecific about that period in her life. She offers only blanket abstractions about the cultural differences between her American self and her Jamaican husband. "Women in Jamaica are very subservient in their marriages," she said in a 1979 interview with Colette Dowling in the *New York Times Magazine*. "They never challenge their husbands. I was a constant nuisance to mine. He didn't need me making judgments about him, which I did."

In later years she would look back on her marriage as a time of emptiness and confusion: "It was as though I had nothing left but my imagination. I had no will, no judgment, no perspective, no power, no authority, no self—just this brutal sense of irony, melancholy and a trembling respect for words." (Century)

(. . . no will, no judgment, no perspective, no power, no authority, no self . . . and a trembling respect for words. There's a whole novel left unsaid.)

She was now a 34-year-old single mother with one child, another on the way, and no job. Depressed and confused, she returned to her parents' home in Lorain, Ohio.

## THE SYRACUSE BLUES

Not long after her second son, Slade Kevin, was born, Toni Morrison left Ohio to take a job as an editor with a textbook subsidiary of Random House in Syracuse, New York. Mornings, she would leave little Harold and Slade with the housekeeper while she went to work. Each evening, like working mothers everywhere, she made dinner for her sons and spent a few hours with them until their bedtime.

Although she lived in Syracuse for two years, Toni Morrison avoided making any friends. The reason she gives is that she was hoping to be transferred to Random House's New York office.

Morrison told Dowling that three things stood out in her memory of the time she spent in Syracuse: hiring a white "maid"; starting (and dropping) a

$200,000 lawsuit against a neighbor for calling her a "tramp" ("That poor woman didn't know what hit her."); and beginning to write.

Work all day, come home every night to care for her sons, no social life, no friends, Morrison found herself growing increasingly depressed. One night, in the deadly hours after she'd put her sons to sleep and the house was quiet, Toni Morrison, friendless for reasons that only she knew, picked up a notebook and began to write. As the words washed through her, cleansing her in some way that she didn't understand, she began to feel that writing might be a way to escape the desperation she felt in this cold city. (A tramp?—Dear God, she didn't even know any men!) As she wrote, the characters she was creating began to take on lives of their own . . . and make demands of their own. They wanted, or seemed to want (as she wondered if she was going crazy for thinking that words on a piece of paper could want anything), the little scrap of story she'd written years ago. So during the cold Syracuse winter of 1967, Toni Morrison dug up the story about the little girl who prayed for blue eyes . . .

What was going on in Morrison's head at the time? Why does a 35-year-old woman suddenly begin writing a novel? From the tone of her interviews, it took Morrison years before she understood her own journey. Ten years later in a conversation with Jane Bakerman, she still sounded mystified:

> I never planned to be a writer. I was in a place where there was nobody I could talk to and have real conversations with. And I think I was also very unhappy. So I wrote then, for that reason.

In 1983, some fifteen years after the fact, she told Claudia Tate:

> I've said I wrote *The Bluest Eye* after a period of depression, but the words "lonely, depressed, melancholy" don't really mean the obvious. They simply represent a different state. . . . The best words for making that state clear to other people are those words. It's not necessarily an unhappy feeling; it's just a different one.
>
>     It happened after my father died. . . . It happened after my divorce. It has happened other times, but not so much because I was unhappy or happy. It was that I was unengaged, and in that situation of disengagement with the day-to-day rush, something positive happened.

At that time I had to be put into it. Now I know how to bring it about without going through the actual event. It's exactly what Guitar said: when you release all the shit, then you can fly.

After working all day as an editor, Morrison would return home each night to her writing. Sometimes she would gaze out the window at the snow and think back to the cold winters of her girlhood in Ohio. Whether her writing was published or not, Morrison knew that she couldn't stop writing this, this . . . novel. She called it *The Bluest Eye.*

Sometimes she would think, "No one is ever going to read this until I'm dead."

## THE BLUEST EYE

*The Bluest Eye* is the story of three black schoolgirls, the sisters Claudia and Frieda McTeer and their friend Pecola Breedlove, growing up in Ohio. Claudia, who tells much of the story, is a strong-willed eight-year-old.

Pecola, her eleven-year-old friend, thinks that her life would be perfect if only she could have blue eyes . . .

### Afterword: New York City

After getting several rejection letters (most of which ended with variations on Great writing, but . . .), Morrison's novel was finally accepted at Holt, Rinehart & Winston. By the time *The Bluest Eye* (1970) was published, TM was living in New York, working as a textbook editor for Random House. She worked her way into the trade division, where she could edit books by black Americans (Muhammad Ali, Andrew Young, Angela Davis, to name a few) and help develop the careers of promising black women writers (Toni Cade Bambara and Gayl Jones). "Toni has done more to encourage and publish other black writers than anyone I know," Andrew Young told *Newsweek* (Strouse).

*The Bluest Eye* wasn't a commercial success, but it did fairly well with the critics. John Leonard, one of the best and bravest book critics in America, went over the edge and raved about *The Bluest Eye* in the *New York Times* (1970). Leonard, in his boundless enthusiasm, praised Morrison for writing "a prose so precise, so faithful to speech and so charged with pain and wonder that the novel becomes poetry." And Liz Gant writing in *Black World,* applauded Morrison for having the courage to address "an aspect of the Black experience that many of us would rather forget, our hatred of ourselves."

Neither TM nor the critics had any idea that she would become one of the premier novelists of our time. But it barely mattered, for Toni Morrison had discovered her magic. Exploring the relationship of three little black girls in Ohio, TM had built them with pieces of her self. "All of those people were me," she said to novelist Gloria Naylor: "I was Pecola, Claudia. . . . I was everybody. And as I began to [write], I began to pick up scraps of things that I had seen or felt, or didn't see or didn't feel, but imagined. And speculated about and wondered about. And I fell in love with myself."

## THROUGH A GLASS DARKLY . . .

Even though her novel wasn't a great success, Toni Morrison was suddenly considered an authority on black cultural issues. Over the next few years, she published several articles and book reviews, mainly in the *New York Times.* But she was getting worried. Months had passed since the publication of *The Bluest Eye* and she didn't have an idea for another book. Maybe that was it—maybe she'd never write fiction again.

It was the early 1970s. The women's liberation movement was gaining ground, but "women's lib" struck TM as so myopically a white middle-class movement that it irritated Morrison into original insight. What irked the hell out of her was the fact that these suddenly enlightened white women had decided that it was time for women to start loving one another, to begin being sisters and friends. What do they mean, begin? All of her life, Toni Morrison had helped, and been helped by, her family and friends. Morrison wondered if black women related to each other differently than white women? She decided to try something that, as far as she knew, had never been done in American fiction: to deeply explore the friendship between two black women.

## SULA

The relationship between Nel Wright and Sula Peace is unique. Even as little girls, they are bound together by a terrible secret. Sula leaves town, returns several years later, and betrays Nel, putting their friendship to the test.

### After Sula

Published in December 1973, *Sula* brought Toni Morrison national recognition. *Sula* was excerpted in *Redbook* and nominated for the 1975 National Book Award in fiction. There was a bit of a controversy when Sara Blackburn wrote in the *New York Times Book Review* that the novel lacked "the stinging immediacy" of Morrison's nonfiction. Alice Walker and several other prominent writers wrote letters of protest to the *Times,* and Morrison herself had a testy response to Blackburn's criticism: "She's talking about my life. It has a stinging immediacy for me." (In fairness to Sara Blackburn, she was not talking about Toni Morrison's life, she was talking about TM's novel and the fictional characters in that novel.) Toni Morrison's thin-skinned defensiveness, coupled with her army of overzealous supporters, will probably end up doing her reputation more harm than her harshest critics. We'll go there later.

Most reviewers were enthusiastic about the book; Toni Morrison was in demand as an "expert" on black life. But sometimes we wondered if the cagey Ms. Morrison was pulling our collective leg: "I went someplace once to talk about *Sula* and there were some genuinely terrified men in the audience, and they walked out and told me why," Morrison told Gloria Naylor. "They said, 'Friendships between women?' Aghast. Really terrified. You wouldn't think anybody grown-up would display his fear quite that way. But it was such a shocking, threatening thing in a book, let alone what it would be in life."

## THE BLACK BOOK

In February 1974, Random House published *The Black Book,* which, according to Bill Cosby's spunky introduction, is the kind of scrapbook we'd have if "a 300-year-old black man had decided, oh, say, when he was about ten, to keep a record of what it was like for himself and his people in these United

States." This anthology of 300 years of African-American life was compiled by Middleton (Spike) Harris and edited and largely inspired by Toni Morrison. Let's stop for a second and consider those two publishing events, one piggy-backing the other, and you'll begin to see why Toni Morrison is, was, and will be one of the most powerfully "impactful" writer/editors in the world:

- In December 1973 her novel *Sula* was published to great critical acclaim.
- Two months later her pet editorial project, *The Black Book,* is published. She hopes it will enable African-Americans to "recognize and rescue those qualities of resistance, excellence, and integrity that were so much a part of our past and so useful to us and to the generations of blacks now growing up" (*New York Times Magazine,* "Rediscovering Black History," 1974).

Toni Morrison is as individualistic and self-absorbed as a fine novelist must be. But when it comes to being an editor, Morrison does not presume to speak for "her" authors or "her" race. She provides, instead, a forum from which they can speak for themselves. As an editor, she seems as proud of her authors' books as she is of her own. *The Black Book* astonished and inspired even her.

As she examined the assortment of newspaper clippings, photos, patents, recipes, and advertisements that made up *The Black Book,* she was reminded of the stories of black achievement that her parents had told her when she was growing up in Ohio:

> I felt a renewal of pride I had not felt since 1941, when my parents told me stories of blacks who had invented airplanes, electricity, and shoes. ("Oh, Mama," I cried, "everybody in the world must have had sense enough to wrap his feet." "I am telling you," she replied, "a Negro invented shoes.") And there it was among Spike Harris's collection of patents: the overshoe. The airplane was also there as an airship registered in 1900 by John Pickering.
>
> —Morrison, "Rediscovering Black History"

Working on *The Black Book,* Morrison was also reminded of the brutality so many black Americans had faced under slavery. She sat in Spike Harris's apartment, reading two- and three-hundred-year-old newspaper accounts of the tortures inflicted upon slaves.

Amid the hideous newspaper clippings she found an 1856 article about a runaway slave who cut the throat of her own daughter rather than see her returned to the slaveholders. Years later, this unthinkable true-life episode would be the inspiration for one of Morrison's most acclaimed novels.

In the meantime, another novel was coming together in Toni Morrison's mind. Her novel *Sula* had received so much attention largely because of its strong female characters . . . so naturally, the in-your-face Ms. Morrison just had to write a novel powered by men . . . or, in her own sometimes overliterary words, a novel "informed by the male spirit."

It was a difficult time in TM's personal life. She had money problems; her oldest son was entering manhood a bit too energetically; and her father died. She went to Ohio for his funeral. After she returned to New York, she couldn't stop thinking about him. As she worked on her new novel, she'd have long conversations with him in her head. She needed his help to write this difficult new book about men.

The result was one of the most astonishing novels of the century . . .

## SONG OF SOLOMON

Macon Dead III—everyone calls him Milkman—leaves his home in Michigan and travels to the South in search of the fabled family fortune, a hidden treasure of gold. Although he never finds the gold, Milkman finds something more important.

*Song of Solomon* is a sweeping epic, much larger than the story of Milkman's quest for his family heritage. Morrison's description of her own book: "It's about black people who could fly."

### The Aftersong

The publication of *Song of Solomon* in 1977 changed Toni Morrison's life. Suddenly—barely out of her teens (technically, she was 46; spiritually, she was a minute past puberty)—Morrison was an "overnight success," both with the critics and with real people. *Song of Solomon* was the first novel by a black writer to become a Book-of-the-Month Club selection since Richard Wright's *Native Son* in 1940. *Song of Solomon* became a paperback bestseller with 570,000 copies in print. Morrison received the National Book Critics Circle Award; she was hailed by critics as a literary giant; and President Jimminy Carter appointed her to the National Council on the Arts.

Not a bad year. Still, despite her success, Morrison continued to work full-time at Random House, teach at Yale every Friday, and be both father and mother for her sons.

Not long after the publication of *Song of Solomon,* TM drove her son Harold to his Manhattan piano lesson. She dropped him off, had an hour to kill, so she drove around Manhattan. She passed a Doubleday bookstore with a large display of books in the window. It took her a few beats to recognize the cover of *Song of Solomon.* She drove around to the other side of the store, also filled with her books, and containing a huge sign, "A Triumph, by Toni Morrison." She sat in the car for a few minutes. It was her they were talking about.

Her? What her? You can be great or beautiful or brilliant or inspiring or sexy or all of the above, but one of the best cuttin-through-the-crap ways of knowing a person (and what is this bio for if it doesn't help us know Toni Morrison?) is to sit in the same room with her. So what is it like to be in a room with Toni Morrison?

(Well, honey, it depends on who you ask.)

Colette Dowling's feature article on Toni Morrison (*New York Times Magazine,* 1979), not only lacked warmth, it was downright bitchy:

> A group called the Friends of Sarah Lawrence Library has sponsored the evening's speaker, which means it has met her rather sizable fee, sent a limousine into Manhattan to fetch her, and wined and dined her in the Tudor mansion of the college president.

A couple hundred words into the article, Mizz Dowling gets down:

> "I have always thought of Toni as a touchy person," one literary critic told me. "She's, well . . . prickly."
>
> I was to learn how prickly she can be. Last spring, we were to meet at the information booth in Grand Central Station 15 minutes before taking the train to Yale, where she was teaching. She appeared about a minute before the train left. Once we'd pushed through the crowded train and found seats, I said, "I waited for you at the information booth."

A dark look flashed from her. "To tell the truth, I wasn't thinking about you at all this morning."

It seemed the better part of wisdom to back off. I took out my *Times,* she took out hers. Sitting opposite each other, our knees almost touching, we remained silent behind our newspapers all the way to New Haven.

In Detroit where I grew up, we'd leave off the LY in "prickly" to describe someone who trashed us like that. But let's don't jump to contusions (after all, Ms. Dowling, despite her air of innocence, may have come on with a bit of attitude and set TM's meters bleeping). Instead, let's compare Dowling's Wicked Witch of the East description of TM with one written by Charles Ruas for *Conversations with American Writers:*

> She is an impressive, strong woman, with an open countenance and a sonorous, melodious voice. Her eyes are amber-colored, of changing golden hue, and her face is extremely expressive, with sudden shifts in tone and mood.
>
> Her response to the questions are direct and forthright; she is eloquent about her beliefs and kindly in her analysis of people. She reserves her mocking humor and caustic wit for comments about herself.

Sounds like a goddess to me.

Once she got past her irritation with Morrison's "assertiveness," Dowling gave TM her due, mentioning that Morrison was featured on the PBS TV series "Writers in America," lecturing everywhere in our solar system, translation rights sold in 11 countries . . .

> And John Leonard didn't exactly hurt the book's chances when, in *The New York Times,* he put it in the same class with . . . Nabokov's *Lolita,* . . . Grass's *The Tin Drum,* and . . . Marquez's *One Hundred Years of Solitude.*

In the meantime, Toni Morrison was thinking, reasoning, ruminating, and researching her way into another novel. It was so different from her other work, so audacious, so . . . No reputable novelist would dare to base a serious literary novel on an old African folk tale that most people know as one of those silly old Uncle Remus stories . . . would they?

(. . . lickety split, lickety split . . .)

## TAR BABY

*Tar Baby*, built on a foundation of black folklore and set on a Caribbean island, is a modern love story between Jadine, a beautiful, pampered black model, and an earthy dreadlocked outlaw named Son.

### The Media Event

America is not a country that makes media stars of its authors. Norman Mailer doesn't have his own line of hundred-dollar Nike sneakers ("Air" Mailers?); nobody asks Joyce Carol Oates to rip her shirt open and say, "I can't believe it's not butter." But Toni Morrison was being peddled like a rock star. Morrison, in her brief career as a novelist, had broken through barriers that limited black writers and women writers, making it infinitely easier for those that followed. Now, with *Tar Baby*, she would break through the commercial/financial/media barriers that had limited *all* writers. Morrison wasn't "just" a writer, she was a celebrity. *Tar Baby* wasn't *just* a book, it was a media event.

Toni Morrison was interviewed and articled by every major newspaper and magazine in the country. She even made an appearance on "The Dick Cavett Show," which was reported by Jean Strouse for *Newsweek:*

> Toward the end of taping a Dick Cavett show, Cavett asks whether it wouldn't have been nice to do the whole show without mentioning the word black. "I guess so," Morrison smiles, "but you started it."

The whole world awaited the new novel by Toni Morrison with such anticipation that you'd have thought they were expecting a new Michael Jackson album.

## SUPERWOMAN!

After the publication of *Tar Baby* in 1981, Toni Morrison finally achieved the ultimate sign of success in America. "Are you really going to put a middle-aged, gray-haired colored lady on the cover of this magazine?" she asked, laughingly.

In March 1981, Toni Morrison became the first black woman ever to appear on the cover of *Newsweek*. America doesn't generally give a serious damn about its writers, no matter what their sex or color, but Morrison was becoming literature's biggest star since Hemingway. After the *Newsweek* cover, virtually all of the major newspapers and magazines in the country featured articles on her. Everyone who interviewed her was amazed by the breadth of her activities: raising two sons, working full-time as an editor, teaching college, writing four novels—they called her Superwoman! In addition to the Superwoman angle, the *Newsweek* story zeroed in on Morrison's impact on other writers. In the words of writer Toni Cade Bambara: "She lures you in, locks the doors and encloses you in a special, very particular universe—all in the first three pages!"

*Tar Baby* was a big success, staying on the bestseller list for four months. But most critics considered it a disappointment after *Song of Solomon*.

(What wouldn't be? *Song of Solomon* was a tough act to follow . . .)

## STARTING OVER AGAIN (AGAIN)

After 20 years of editorship during which Morrison presided over some of the seminal moments of the African-American literary revolution of the 1970s, Morrison left Random House in 1983. In 1984, she was named Albert Schweitzer Professor of the Humanities at the State University of New York in Albany. Her main job was to conduct fiction workshops for young writers. It almost goes without saying Morrison's students describe her as "inspiring," "conscientious," "brilliant," "so down-to-earth."

Something about upstate New York seemed to get her juices flowing.

It was in Albany that Morrison began working on her first play.

## DREAMING EMMETT

Emmett Till was a black Chicago teenager who, while visiting his uncle in Mississippi in 1955, was accused of whistling at a white woman. Fourteen-year-old Emmett Till was kidnapped, shot in the head, and thrown into a river. The white men charged with his murder were acquitted by an all-white jury. Because of its flagrant brutality and injustice, the Emmett Till murder became a rallying point for the Civil Rights movement. In Morrison's stage play, *Dreaming Emmett,* Emmett Till was allowed to speak on his own behalf. He was brought back from the dead to describe his murder in his own words, from his point of view.

## IT BELONGED TO LIFE, NOT ART

Morrison's next major work also had its origins in a violent historical incident—the story of the woman she had read about while doing research for *The Black Book.* In 1851, a slave named Margaret Garner escaped from her master in Kentucky and fled with her four children to a small neighborhood outside Cincinnati, Ohio. When she was tracked down by her master's slave catchers, Margaret Garner tried to kill her children so that they would not be returned to the humiliating life of slavery.

For years after reading about that woman, Morrison wanted to write her story but she couldn't. It wouldn't come out. Morrison decided that the story simply couldn't be written. It belonged to life, not to art. Then she wrote it.

## *Beloved*

Sethe is struggling to create a new life for herself in Ohio, despite the fact that her house is haunted by the ghost of the baby she killed some eighteen years earlier. Paul D. (a former slave) tries to cast out the baby's spirit and seems to have succeeded until one day a beautiful twenty-year-old stranger with a scar on her throat arrives at Sethe's house . . .

### Hardballing Beloved

*Beloved* (1987), an immediate best seller, was quickly acclaimed as Morrison's most powerful book. Walter Clemmons, writing in *Newsweek,* called *Beloved* "a magnificent novel . . . profoundly imagined and carried out with burning fervor." Novelist Margaret Atwood wrote in the *New York Times Book Review* that Morrison's "versatility and technical and emotional range appear to know no bounds."

Despite its acclaim, *Beloved* failed to win either the National Book Award or the National Book Critics Circle Award. In January 1988, forty-nine black writers and critics, outraged by the lack of official recognition given Morrison's novel, published a signed tribute to her achievements in the *New York Times Book Review.* The letter mentioned that James Baldwin had never received the National Book Award or the Pulitzer Prize and chastised the good old boys on the committees for their "oversight and harmful whimsy" in not giving either award to Morrison.

Some critics viewed the letter as an attempt to intimidate the Pulitzer Prize committee; others, including the brilliant novelist Ralph Ellison, felt that, if *Beloved* were awarded the Pulitzer Prize for fiction, the novel's brilliance would be tainted by the controversy surrounding the "manifesto."

On March 31, 1988, *Beloved* won the Pulitzer Prize. Morrison (who sometimes sounds like the CEO of Morrison, Inc.) said "I am certain they [the letter writers] played no significant role in the judgment." Her formal statement was just as disingenuous: "I am glad that the merits of the book were allowed to surface and be the only consideration of the Pulitzer Prize committee" *(Century).* Toni Morrison, at age fifty-seven, had become not only one of the world's great novelists, but one of its foremost bullslingers. (Author's note: That's how I felt before I read *Beloved.* After I read the novel, I "modified" my reaction. The new version is in the chapter on *Beloved,* but it seemed important to leave this one in. As Toni Morrison shows us again and again in her novels, what seems right one minute is wrong the next.)

In 1989, Toni Morrison became the first black woman to hold a named chair (the Robert F. Goheen Professor in the Council of Humanities) at an Ivy League university (Princeton). Princeton was in the process of building one of the country's leading African-American studies programs, attracting Morrison and leading black scholars like Cornel West and Arnold Rampersand. In addition to teaching creative writing at Princeton, Morrison was actively involved in the African-American studies, American studies, and women's studies departments.

And in her spare time, she began work on another novel.

Years before she thought of writing *Beloved,* Toni Morrison had seen a book by the photographer James Van Der Zee. *The Harlem Book of the Dead* was a collection of photographs of dead black New Yorkers taken in the 1920s.

One of the photographs especially intrigued Toni Morrison: it was a picture of a dead girl lying in a coffin. The text that accompanied the photo explained that the girl, who was eighteen years old, had been dancing at a "rent party" when she was shot.

## <u>Jazz</u>

Joe Trace, a middle-aged salesman, falls crazy in love with Dorcas, an 18-year-old girl "with one of those deepdown, spooky loves that . . . he had to shoot her just to keep the feeling going." Joe's wife crashes the funeral and tries to cut the dead girl's face with a butcher knife.

Meanwhile, in her other spare time, TM had taken a series of lectures she'd given at Harvard and turned them into a book. Nonfiction hardball . . .

### *Playing in the Dark with Whitey*

Using examples of American fiction from Poe to Hemingway, Morrison argues that black language and culture have played a much stronger role in American literature than most white writers admit. She titled her pugnacious little book *Playing in the Dark: Whiteness and the Literary Imagination.*

Both *Jazz* and *Playing in the Dark* were published early in 1992. Despite their obvious dissimilarities, the two books were often reviewed together. In contrast to the overwhelming critical acclaim for *Beloved,* the response to *Jazz* was disappointing. The book did get some good reviews, even some great ones. John Leonard, in a looong, breathless, beautiful rumination (in the *Nation,* 1992) on Morrison's career, said what he always says—Toni Morrison is simply "the best writer working in America." Henry Louis Gates, Jr., one of the finest critics around, argues ingeniously (in *Toni Morrison: Critical Perspectives Past and Present*) that Morrison "composed" *Jazz*-the-novel in precisely the way Ellington composed music—for each player's unique sound: "Like Duke Ellington, Morrison has found a way, paradoxically, to create an ensemble of improvised sound out of a composed music."

But the bad reviews drowned out the good ones: Edna O'Brien, the fine Irish novelist, writing in the almost too influential *New York Times Book Review,* had some praise for *Jazz,* but ultimately, she felt that the characters never really came to life.

The critical response to *Playing in the Dark* was even less enthu—downright brutal. Ann Hulbert, in the *New Republic,* referred to Morrison's "blissful ignorance of the politicized academic climate" and Bruce Bawer, in the *New Criterion,* said that Morrison had "absolutely nothing original to say." (I guess they didn't like it!)

If the critics thought that their harsh treatment would shut Morrison up, they were wrong. In the fall of the same year (1992), TM edited and wrote an introduction to a collection of essays titled (get ready for this) *Race-ing Justice, En-gendering Power: Essays on Anita Hill, Clarence Thomas, and the Construction of Social Reality.* In her introduction, Toni Morrison put forth the unremarkable opinion that Clarence Thomas had subjugated his black identity to make it in white America.

Despite the bad reviews, everyone seemed to want an opinion from TM on everything. She didn't disappoint them: She was a veritable opinion factory, sharing her muscular views on everything from the Rodney King riots to teen pregnancy.

In the spring of 1993, TM did a one-hour interview on "The Charlie Rose Show," a nationally televised public TV program. Midway through the interview, Rose, a smart, fairly sensitive white dude from North Carolina, quoted a remark made by the late tennis star Arthur Ashe that living with AIDS was easier than living with racism. Rose (who, for a smart guy, is sometimes too pleased with himself for asking dumb questions) asked Morrison if she still encountered racism (!!!). Morrison (who, for a brilliant woman, sometimes delivers lame answers as if she were giving the Wisdom of the Ages) started into a speech that was about as memorable as two foul balls. Then, when Charlie Rose asked her about her work at Princeton, Morrison hit a home run: "If you study the culture and art of African-Americans, you are not studying a regional or minor culture," she said. "What you are studying is America."

On October 7, 1993, the Nobel Committee of the Swedish Academy announced that Toni Morrison had won the 1993 Nobel Prize in Literature.

## SUPERWOMAN IN STOCKHOLM

When Toni Morrison arrived in Stockholm, she was met at the airport by herds of reporters. The well-meaning Swedes, whose English is good—but not that good—asked her if she thought that her winning the Nobel Prize would "improve racism" in the United States. She was dying to say, "Of course not; it's perfect as it is," but she's a gracious lady who doesn't take cheap shots.

Morrison's speech to the Swedish Academy was so good that (according to John Leonard, writing in the *Nation* (1994)— who also happened to spill the beans on TM for not applauding Barbara Hendricks) "it inspired from Darnton [*New York Times*] and Robinson [*Washington Post*] dispatches of such warmth and grace their editors must have won-

... who *usually* doesn't take cheap shots: The Swedes, in an obvious attempt to honor Toni Morrison, imported Barbara Hendricks, a young African-American soprano with an almost supernaturally beautiful voice to sing at the ceremony. Unfortunately, Morrison refused to applaud after Ms. Hendricks's "astonishing version of 'Summertime.'" I'm no Gershwin fan; I badmouthed him in two separate genres (I wrote a book on opera and another on jazz) and I agree with TM's objection to the idiotic cartooning of black English (da fish iz jumpin an de cotton iz high)—but I passionately disagree with TM's public embarrassment of a young black artist who could have learned the same lesson with a private word from Toni Morrison.

dered what mushrooms they'd been munching in the Stockholm dark." Leonard went on to say that "for the first time in the memory of the Foreign Ministry, the audience, unable to help itself, stood for a second standing ovation."

She was the eighth woman—the first black woman—to win the Nobel Prize in Literature. When Toni Morrison, arm in arm with the King of Sweden, led the Nobel procession, John Leonard wrote: "I wasn't the only wet-eyed New York smarty-pants proud to be a citizen of whatever country Toni Morrison comes from."

## The Aftermath

On Christmas morning, less than two weeks after she'd accepted the Nobel Prize, Toni Morrison's house caught fire and burned to the ground. She wasn't hurt, but most of her original manuscripts were destroyed. She was shattered, but with the same indomitable will that carried her ancestors through every imaginable horror, she fought her way through her depression and went to work on a new novel.

The new novel was inspired by an obscure bit of American history. After the Civil War, groups of former slaves went into the sparsely populated Western states that we usually identify with American cowboys to set up all-black towns. The all-black towns put ads in newspapers seeming to invite black people to join the new communities . . . with the enigmatic warning, "Come Prepared or Not at All."

During the writing of the novel, which was six years in the making, Toni Morrison was taken up as a Sacred Cause by Oprah Winfrey. Oprah promoted TM's books on her influential book club, began making a movie of *Beloved* (produced by and starring Oprah), and bought the rights to Morrison's new novel *Paradise*.

## Paradise

The isolated, past-obsessed citizens of the all-black town of Ruby, Oklahoma, project their faults and blame their problems on the women who live in "the Convent," a mansion on the outskirts of town: "They shoot the white girl first. With the rest they can. . . ."

### You never saw so many reviews in your life!

Two reviews in the *New York Times!*
A page and a half in the *New York Times Book Review!*
A seven-page cover story in *Time!*
Five pages in the *New Yorker!*
Three and a half pages in the *Nation!*
A full page in *Newsweek!*
A two-page interview in *Essence!*
A full hour TV interview with Charlie Rose!
A 20-minute rap with Ed Bradley on "60 Minutes"!

And, of course, there were dozens of cute little reviews in places like *Library Journal, Booklist, Time Out New York,* Chicago newspapers, Detroit newspapers, Philadelphia and Baltimore newspapers. In January (1998), there were reviews of (or articles about) *Paradise* in just about every magazine and newspaper I came across.

## What did the reviews say?

They were so mixed you wondered if they'd all read the same book: The novel was murdered in the daily *New York Times* and praised in the *Times Book Review;* it was referred to as her most accessible book in one review and her most complex in another. Most enthusiastic reviews seemed either very naive or more willed than genuine.

But do you know the weirdest part?

None, absolutely none, of the first wave of reviewers noticed what's really going on in the novel. All those brilliant people in all those prestigious publications misunderstood the book completely. *Paradise* is one of the most fascinating novels ever written.

But they didn't get it.

*Our past was appropriated. I am one of the people who has to reappropriate it.*
—TONI MORRISON, *CONVERSATIONS WITH TONI MORRISON*

*Forget about what I say in an interview*
*—it might be anything—*
*but trust the tale and start with that.*
—TONI MORRISON TO KATHY NEUSTADT, 1980

# HER NOVELS

## A SENSE OF PROPORTION

Literary criticism can be done brilliantly or badly or anything in between, but even when it's done brilliantly, it's small potatoes next to the book it criticizes. The least of Toni Morrison's novels is a greater gift to life than anything I or anyone else can say about it. A novel adds to life; our words merely comment on it. We are (ugh!) Howard Cosell to her Muhammad Ali. So I will say what every critic should say before he presumes the right to judge another person's labor of love: "Thank you. I will try not to lose sight of the fact that you have done all the work and taken all the risks."

### Judging TM on Her Own Terms

One thing that Toni Morrison asks of her readers is to meet her books on their own terms. Instead of judging her books by standards that don't fit, she wants us to understand her standards, her goals. What are her goals? Her overarching goal is to write the kind of book she'd like to read—a uniquely African-American version of the novel. She would say, trying not to offend earlier black writers, that the novels that had been written by black people (especially men) were essentially "Eurocentric" novels about black people. What would this African-Americanized novel be like? Morrison names eleven characteristics that she feels should define African-American writing:

1. A participatory quality between book and reader. She wants you IN the story, not on the outside looking in.
2. An aural quality in the writing—writing like spoken words instead of written words.
3. An open-endedness in the endings of her books that is agitating—no tidy little endings that tie everything into a neat package.
4. An acceptance of and ability to detect differences—don't *homogenize* everything.
5. Acknowledgment of a broader cosmology and system of logic—one that includes magic and mystery and listens to the body when it speaks.
6. A functional as well as an aesthetic quality. For example, a jazz funeral march is functional: it isn't *just* music; it honors the dead and connects the living to their ancestors. (We'll look at examples as they occur in the novels; they'll make more sense.)
7. An obligation to bear witness.
8. Service as a conduit for the *ancestor.*
9. Uses of humor that are frequently ironic.
10. An achieved clarity or epiphany and a tendency to be prophetic.
11. A novel that would take her people through the pain and denial of their racially haunted history to a healing zone.

## SHOULD YOU JUDGE MORRISON'S NOVELS ON HER TERMS . . . OR YOURS?

You should listen with an open mind to what she has to say; you should have a clear understanding of what she's trying to accomplish; then you should forget everybody's terms, rules, and theories (including hers, your own, and mine) and read her books with a completely open mind. Nine times out of ten, whether you love a novel or not won't have anything to do with whose theory you vote for. Judge her books according to your own sense of beauty, logic, and meaning. Don't let anyone, including Toni Morrison (or me) talk you into loving something you don't.

On the other hand, if TM's mission to create a uniquely African-American novel makes you fret that her books may be less en-

> You can't understand TM's objection to the Eurocentric novel unless you have some idea what the Euro novel is—so I'll fill you in on that as we go along. (We'll also see why the Eurocentric point of view is actually AFROcentric!)

joyable or less beautiful to non-black readers—nothing could be further from the truth. Morrison's books will thrill, irritate, and sanctify anyone who gives them a chance. And if she does succeed in creating a truly African-American novel, like jazz, a truly African-American music, it will give people of every color options and ecstasies we never had before.

## IS THERE ANYTHING WE SHOULD KNOW ABOUT THIS BOOK OR ITS APPROACH?

It might help you to know WHO it's written to or for: to be perfectly blunt, I have tried to write a book that would be accessible enough for the most naive, inexperienced, scared-shitless-of-books readers and challenging enough for some of the smartest people in the world: the professors, critics, reviewers, and others who help shape the reading public's attitude. The only way I could imagine combining those seemingly exclusive goals was to write a book that's such a pleasure to read that its momentum will carry smart people through the naive parts and naive people through the smart parts and (the gods willing) make naive readers curious enough to look things up on their own. And if I engage the professors on creative issues instead of pedantic ones, the kids will get the gist of what's going down even if some of the details get past them.

Whether I've pulled it off or not isn't for me to decide. (But I came pretty close.)

I have challenged both TM's critics and her disciples by offering different viewpoints (sometimes drastically different) on her work than I've seen anywhere. Of course, an introductory book should also present the conventional viewpoint, so I've done that as well. Generally, I think that both her critics and her fans have been far too influenced by what Toni Morrison says about her own work. (Would you settle for Mr. Clinton's assessment of his two terms as president?) Critics and fans alike, we're challenging you to RE-read TM's books!

> SIDEBARS in general contain details or specialized info that some of you will consider the best part of this book and others will want to skip.
>
> Let your own goals and curiosity guide you.

More than most intros to novels, this book will try to explain what novelists do and how novels work for the general reader (I'm amazed at how little people know about how novels work). I will also try to clarify what Toni Morrison does so that aspiring novelists can try to apply it to their work. (Good luck, sweet pea!)

## Anything Else That Sets This Book Apart from Others in the Field?

Yes. Its HUMOR, its complete HONESTY, and the fact that it's SPOKEN. (Spoken?)

- HUMOR: Toni Morrison is in grave danger of being treated like a sacred cow. I have done my best to remedy that.
- HONESTY: During the writing of this book, I asked dozens of people this question: Should I be completely honest? Every one of them answered with an emphatic YES.

If you aren't certain that you want a completely honest book on Toni Morrison, do us both a favor and switch to one of the books that fawn over every word she's written. Just don't come whining at me if you can't handle what I say.

My approach is so straightforward and so devoid of crap that you might wonder how anyone could have trouble with it: Toni Morrison is the author of seven novels of drastically varying quality. The way I see it, she's written three and a half of the best novels in the world, a couple of pretty klunky novels, and one or two that are half-and-half. (If anything, history will be less generous than I have been, not more.)

■ SPOKEN? I thought this book would be more fun to read, less intimidating to inexperienced readers, and, in the process, help convey the spirit of Morrison's books—if it was written in the rhythms of spoken English, just as she writes her novels.

Now, for those of you who are new to TM's novels, let's take notice of a few general things to look out for that will help you enjoy and understand her books.

## A Few Things to Be on the Lookout For

Pay attention to names. Although she is sometimes as unsubtle as Charles Dickens when it comes to naming, Toni Morrison doesn't name anyone or anything casually. She names neighborhoods (The Bottom), streets (Not Doctor Street), houses (124) with wit or foreboding; her characters have startlingly beautiful Biblical names (First Corinthians), impersonal "generic" names (Son, Old Man), cartoon names (Chicken Little), ironic names (Tar Baby for a white guy, President Lincoln for a horse), and names out of Roman history (Seneca) or Greek mythology (Circe, Pallas). Two points to note:

Every black American whose ancestors were taken from Africa by force has been robbed of his family name. That was no accident; you enslave a person's spirit by wiping out her identity; your name—and your family name—are badges of your identity. The slavers did everything they could to remove those badges (breaking up families, tribes, language groups, selling children), so an African-American, free at last, is a person in search of his name.

Keep an open mind: names don't always mean what they seem to mean. Example: people familiar with Greek mythology will recognize the name Pallas as Athena (the Greek goddess of wisdom); but not many people know that Pallas is also a breed of cat, so they'll miss the foolish humor when people say to Pallas (in TM's novel *Paradise*) "Here, pussy." And if you let your mind close too quickly, you won't see that Pallas's main function is to nudge you into making a creative leap over her name to the book(s) *Black Athena*. Stay curious, stay open. TM's novels are filled with hidden treasures, many of which are connected to names.

Be aware of HUMOR. Most discussions of Toni Morrison's work sound as if they were taking place in a cathedral. That's too bad, because all that reverence is liable to rob you of one of the great pleasures of Morrison's writing: the woman is FUNNY.

Mrs. Baines's opinion of a "Negro" in business, Mr. Smith's suicide note, the beauty parlor lady's assessment of Milkman's and Hagar's relationship in *Song of Solomon* are hilarious, ridiculous, sad, grim. Virtually everything that One Legged Eva (in *Sula*) says and thinks is tilted in some brilliant comic way; and the bit about the Three Deweys is one of the most wonderfully whacko hunks of writing I've ever seen.

Even in *Beloved,* after all that anguish, one stupid little joke reaffirms life.

Screw the reverence. Relax and let Toni Morrison's humor come through.

These are good OLD-FASHIONED novels. Toni Morrison is well known as a (choose one or all of the following) poetic, black, American, female, Faulknerian, magical realist—but one of the most satisfying things about her novels is seldom noted: in many ways, they are very old-fashioned. Modern novels are spare, economical, streamlined; the modern author denies his own flesh, aspires to be a tape recorder or a video camera, and has no opinions, no thoughts, no digressions, and no dialogue over four words long.

Toni Morrison's novels have too much of everything: too many characters, too many digressions, too much symbolism, too many flowery descriptions, and the author has the ovaries (is that the female equivalent of "balls"?) to actually express her opinions. I think that many of Toni Morrison's novels are flawed by any standard of novel writing, but even then they are satisfying in ways that "modern" novels are not. Modern novels are like tasteful, ergonomically designed plastic furniture; Toni Morrison's novels are made of four-inch-thick oak with fatass pillows covered with colorful clashing prints and whorehouse-red velvet with fringes, carved animal claws for feet, buttons on the pillows that poke you in the ass, substantial, hand-made, ornate—elegance and bad taste side by side—and God only knows what you're liable to find hiding beneath the pillows. Satisfying. In ways, more like Dickens than Faulkner.

She STRADDLES HISTORY. Just about every Toni Morrison novel has elements that strike me as ridiculously incongruent, as if she put a frog's head on an elephant. A typical example: she'll have a dozen different narrators (suggesting a sort of "post-Faulkner" modernism), but one of her narrators will be the Author Lecturing Her Readers (a technique that's been scorned and despised since Fielding did it in the early eighteenth century). Or she'll give us a squirt of dialogue so real and racy that she must've tape-recorded it last week in my old Detroit neighborhood . . . Then she'll veer off into a hyper-poetic whipped cream description of autumn leaves that makes the 19th-century romance ladies sound like Ernest Hemingway. (What's she serve for dinner—meatloaf and old socks?)

That incongruity annoyed me for over a year . . . Then one day I remembered jazz critic Martin Gayford's description of legendary bassist/composer Charles Mingus: "Mingus straddled history." Mingus's music reached backward into jazz's past and forward into jazz's future, while completely ignoring—"straddling"—jazz's present. Suddenly Toni Morrison's apparent incongruities made perfect sense: she straddles history. She's as old-fashioned as Fielding and Dickens and as modern as Faulkner and Joyce—and she ignores damn near everything in between.

Whether it's a conscious choice or the way her soul is shaped, who knows? But if you get a feeling that is the book-reading equivalent of wondering if your shoes are on the wrong feet (or in extreme cases, like you switched novels), just remind yourself, Toni Morrison straddles history. She goes from the past to the future without even bothering to stop in the present.

Before we move out of this intro and into TM's first novel, there is one more question we should ask. If you want to experience the full impact of the roller coaster ride a good Morrison novel can take you on, it's the most important question of all.

## HOW WOULD TONI MORRISON LIKE US TO READ HER NOVELS?

Charles Ruas asked Toni Morrison that question in a 1981 interview. Her answer was challenging to say the least:

> I would like to . . . put the reader into the position of being naked and quite vulnerable. . . . Let him make up his mind about what he likes and what he thinks and what happened based on the very intimate acquaintance with the people in the book.

*It wasn't that easy being a little black girl in this country—it was rough. The psychological tricks you have to play in order to get through—and nobody said how it felt to be that.*
—Toni Morrison to Gloria Naylor

*We substituted good grammar for intellect; we switched habits to simulate maturity; we rearranged lies and called it truth.*
—The Bluest Eye

# The Bluest Eye
## *(1970)*

## BACKGROUND

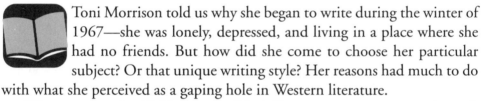 Toni Morrison told us why she began to write during the winter of 1967—she was lonely, depressed, and living in a place where she had no friends. But how did she come to choose her particular subject? Or that unique writing style? Her reasons had much to do with what she perceived as a gaping hole in Western literature.

Westerners are justifiably proud of their literature—over 500 years' worth of some of the finest writing in the world—but imagine for a moment what that fine wall of books feels like to a writer of color. To a black writer, Western literature is like a 500-year-long Woody Allen movie: there's a whole lot of wonderful "stuff" in there . . . but where'd they put the damned black people?

What struck Morrison as almost more tragic than the literal absence of black people in Western literature was the fact that the black Americans whose books she had read (mostly men: Richard Wright, Ralph Ellison, James Baldwin) seemed as if they were always writing to a white audience, explaining things about black culture that they would never have to explain to her if they were sitting around over coffee. In the plainest, simplest terms, Toni Morrison wanted to write a book about black people, in the language of black people, without having to look over her shoulder to explain her world to white people. The example she likes to give is the opening of *The Bluest Eye:* " 'Quiet as it's kept, there were no marigolds in the fall of 1941.' To white people, 'Quiet as it's kept' means . . . 'Quiet as it's kept.' . . . but to black people," Morrison explained, "it means a big lie is about to be told. Or someone is going to tell some graveyard information, who's sleeping with whom. Black readers will chuckle." (Thomas LeClair, *New Republic*)

Although there had been black women writers before her—she'd heard of Zora Neale Hurston, Lorraine Hansberry, Gwendolyn Brooks—she knew very little about them; they weren't being taught in the universities. So, setting out to write *The Bluest Eye,* Toni Morrison felt that she was alone in wanting to express the world of the black people she'd grown up with. Above all, she wanted to talk about the people who were always in the background—like little girls. Little black girls. Toni wondered if she was the only person in the world who thought it was important to tell their story.

During the winter of 1967, Martin Luther King, Jr., and his coworkers were marching to desegregate the South; TM's former student, Stokely Carmichael, was raising hell as a leader of the Student Nonviolent Coordinating Committee; and everywhere you turned people were talking with great pride about some wonderful new thing called Black Power. Despite all the excitement and hype generated by the mere mention of Black Power, Morrison wasn't buying it: "Whatever was going on, was not about me. . . . Nobody was going to tell me that it had been that easy. That all I needed was a slogan: 'Black is Beautiful.' It wasn't that easy being a little black girl in this country—it was rough. The psychological tricks you have to play in order to get through—and nobody said how it felt. . . ." (Gloria Naylor)

Perhaps nothing hammered home what it meant to be "a little black girl in this country" like an "experiment" that made headlines in the 1960s. Little black girls were shown drawings of little girls of varying color and asked to rate the girls in the pictures. The children were very discriminating: they picked up on the most subtle differences in eye, hair, and skin color and arranged the pictures in a near-perfect hierarchy of light to dark. They were also consistent. In nearly every case, the little girls—the little black girls—rated the blondest, lightest-skinned, bluest-eyed girls as the prettiest, smartest, nicest, and best little girls in the world.

I'm sure it was just a coincidence, but not long after that, there were riots in nearly every major city in America. And there was a novel, *The Bluest Eye.* It had a few flaws, which gave you an excuse to ignore it if you couldn't handle what it said.

Correction: It didn't say—it SANG.

### The Image

If you take away all the detours, digressions, bios, flashbacks, meditations on nature, pontifications on human nature, and writing so outrageously beautiful you want to kiss the page . . . if you remove all that and cut to the heart of the novel, *The Bluest Eye* is the story of Pecola Breedlove—No!—it's not the *story* of Pecola Breedlove, it is the *image* of Pecola Breedlove, an eleven-year-old black girl who thinks her life would be perfect if only she had blue eyes. That image in itself is so powerful that it sums up one of the great tragedies of our age in the time it takes to snap your fingers.

Let's talk about the story . . . or the book?

> **Psst!**
>
> I'm only going to say this once, but it applies to each of TM's novels: if you haven't read *The Bluest Eye,* but you're ready to try it, read it now—then come back to this section. You're better off reading the novel first and getting your own soul's reaction without me or anyone else in the middle. When you're finished, come back and compare your reaction to mine and write me to tell me how full of crap I was.

## THE STORY OR THE BOOK?

In a Toni Morrison novel, there's a big difference between the story and the book. I'll tell you the story in two pages, but you still won't have a solid idea what the book is like. *The Bluest Eye* is the story of three black schoolgirls growing up in 1940s Ohio, the sisters Claudia and Frieda MacTeer and their friend Pecola Breedlove. Claudia and Frieda's parents are strict, protective, and when they have time—which isn't often—loving. Pecola is ignored by her mother and abused by her father. Claudia, who tells much of the story, is a strong-willed eight-year-old black girl who can't stand the sight of little blond-haired, blue-eyed dolls. When she's given one for Christmas, her reaction cuts through the pretense: "What was I supposed to do with it? Pretend I was its mother?"

Then she rips it to pieces, trying to discover what there was about that hard little pink thing that everyone seemed to find so lovable. The strong-minded Claudia can't stand the sight of the child movie star Shirley Temple, with her golden curls and baby-blue eyes. (If you haven't read the novel, I won't deprive you of the pleasure of discovering for yourself why Claudia hates Shirley Temple.) Eleven-year-old Pecola idolizes Shirley Temple, loves drinking milk out of Claudia's Shirley Temple cup, and loves eating Mary Janes, the epoxy-like penny candies with the Shirley Temple clone on the wrapper. Pecola is lonely and sad. Her classmates tease her constantly, telling her she is ugly, or singsonging at her that her father's a drunk who sleeps naked.

Pecola, utterly clueless about the war raging inside her, thinks that her life would be perfect if only she could have blue eyes. In one especially poignant scene, Pecola had begun to menstruate earlier in the day. Neither she nor Claudia had the vaguest notion what that meant; but Frieda, who was a couple years older than Claudia, knew:

That night, in bed, the three of us lay still. We were full of awe and respect for Pecola. Lying next to a real person who was ministratin' was somehow sacred. She was different from us now—grown-up like. She, herself, felt the distance but refused to lord it over us.

After a long while she spoke very softly. "Is it true that I can have a baby now?"

"Sure," said Frieda drowsily. "Sure you can."

"But . . . how?" Her voice was hollow with wonder.

"Oh," said Frieda, "someone has to love you."

"Oh."

There was a long pause in which Pecola and I thought this over. It would involve, I suppose, "My man," who, before leaving me, would love me. But there weren't any babies in the songs my mother sang. Maybe that's why the women were sad: the men left before they could make a baby.

Then Pecola asked a question that had never entered my mind. "How do you do that? I mean, how do you get someone to love you?" But Frieda was asleep. And I didn't know.

Pecola is raped by her drunken father and becomes pregnant with his child. As her pregnancy begins to show, instead of being sympathetic, Pecola's mother beats her and forbids her to go to school. When the baby is born prematurely and dies, Pecola loses what little grip on reality she had and begins to go mad. Desperate and confused, she visits a West Indian preacher called Soaphead Church to see if he can give her the blue eyes she's always wanted. Soaphead, an unscrupulous creep who's almost crazy enough to believe in his own "miracles," tells Pecola that God will give her blue eyes, but that she'll

> **The THEME of the novel is strong, clear, and important enough to die from:**
>
> Every black person in America is forced to struggle against a standard of beauty—and by implication (beauty is never just beauty), everything else, from goodness to worthiness of love—that is almost exactly the opposite of what they are . . . and the consequences can be deadly.
>
> The novel suggests that the oppressive standard of beauty peddled by movies and advertisements ravages white self-esteem as well . . . but it isn't just a matter of degree. Low self-esteem is an entirely different creature than self-hate.

be the only one who can see them. By the end of the book, Pecola is talking to an imaginary friend, asking over and over if her eyes are the bluest of all.

## THAT'S THE STORY, NOW LET'S TALK ABOUT THE BOOK

A young black girl wants blue eyes, is raped by her father, goes crazy, and dies. It's a strong little story, but it doesn't begin to suggest the power the novel carries. It's the form of the novel—the way the story is told, the way the pieces are arranged, and what that arrangement implies—that generates the novel's power.

If you aren't used to "experimental novels," the layout of *The Bluest Eye* might shake you up a little at first. (TM insists that she is not an experimental novelist: [1] Some of us disagree with her. [2] In 1970 when she wrote *The Bluest Eye,* everyone was an experimental novelist.)

*The Bluest Eye* has three different beginnings. The *first* beginning—the opening words of the novel—is a slice out of one of those Dick-and-Jane books that so many of us learned to read on.

Here is the house. It is green and white. It has a red door. It is very pretty. Here is the family. Mother, Father, Dick, and Jane live in the green and white house. They are very happy.
—the opening words of *The Bluest Eye*

The Dick-and-Jane primer makes several points (without mentioning them directly) before you know what hit you: every child in America grows up on Dick and Jane, every child in America aspires to be Dick and Jane, compares herself to Dick and Jane (who, in case you haven't noticed, are blond-haired, blue-eyed, and as white as it gets). What happens if you can't stop measuring yourself against Dick and Jane?

The mild version is a lack of self-esteem.

The medium version is self-hate.

The queen-sized version is Pecola Breedlove.

On page two, the soul-shrinking Dick-and-Jane story has degenerated into chaos. The letters run together into one, long, ugly, meaningless, word—

". . . willplaywithjanetheywillplayagoodgameplayjaneplay"

That only lasts a few lines and you don't have to read it to get the point. But what Toni Morrison managed to pull off in little more than a page was to "tell" the story of her entire novel in microcosm. (I think it's a great way to begin a book; some of the critics didn't.) That's over in a page and a half.

*The Bluest Eye*'s second beginning is a one-page "gossip" in which Claudia (who is now a grown woman looking back on the story) gives us just enough info for us to beg her to tell us the rest of the story. (Morrison's intention is to give her novel the feeling that you're sitting there over coffee, listening to a story—not reading it.) Most novels are essentially mysteries—you read them to find out what happens. That's not the case with *The Bluest Eye*. Claudia tell us the punch line on the first real page of the book:

Quiet as it's kept, there were no marigolds in the fall of 1941. We thought, at the time, that it was because Pecola was having her father's baby that the marigolds did not grow.

A few lines later we learn that, by the time we're being told the story (several years after the fact), Pecola, her baby, and her father are all dead. We also know that the story took place between the Autumn of 1940 and the Autumn of '41. Since we already know what happened, we read the book to find out why . . . or in this case, "since why is difficult to handle" you find out "how."

*The Bluest Eye*'s third beginning (the "regular" story) begins on page three. The novel (beginning with Autumn) is divided into sections that correspond to the seasons. Morrison's novels never forget their connection to nature, to the seasons, to the past. In the words of Barbara Christian "Wind and fire, robins as a plague in the spring, marigolds that won't sprout, are as much characterizations in her novels as the human beings who people them." In the seasons that follow, Claudia (grown-up version) introduces the action, time, place, and characters and sets the tone for the scenes and chapters within that season. Much of the time, Claudia doesn't say "I," she says "we," speaking for herself and her sister—and in a very important sense, speaking for

### Linear

Most novels, movies, and plays are linear—they go in a straight line; somebody wants something; they try to get it; they overcome one obstacle, which causes another; they overcome (or don't) that obstacle . . . and so on, until they do (or don't) get what they want. The End.

### Circular or Cyclic

A book designed around the seasons is telling you something right off: this book is not linear (it doesn't have a beginning & end), it's circular, part of an ongoing process. A season book that opens in autumn is telling you something else. Spring is a time of rebirth; autumn is a time when things die. A novel that opens in autumn isn't likely to be a cheery book. That's the bad news; the good news is that a book that rhymes with the seasons is telling you that, as bad as things seem, it isn't final; it's part of a cycle; hang in there till Spring.

### Doubling

Writers often work in Twos or "Pairs" so they can compare & contrast. The most common version is contrasting pairs (Jekyll & Hyde, night & day, Good & Evil). Some contrasting pairs in *The Bluest Eye*: Dick-&-Jane fantasy & Pecola's reality? Pecola buys into white standard of beauty & Claudia fights it? Pecola's drab house & Geraldine's tidy house? Pecola & Shirley Temple. Related terms: twinning, doppelgänger.

us. (Remember, one of TM's goals is to bring us into the book, to make us participants instead of mere observers.)

Morrison also begins each chapter with a piece of the Dick-and-Jane primer, usually in contrast to the story that follows (e.g., comparing Dick-and-Jane's "pretty house" with Pecola's shabby house. TM likes to use Contrasting Pairs & other kinds of DOUBLING.

Claudia's section ends; the next section begins with a few run-together words from Dick and Jane, then the story is told by an omniscient (all-knowing) narrator who can go backward and forward in time and place and can jump in and out of anyone's consciousness. In these sections, we learn the backgrounds of other characters: Mr. and Mrs. Breedlove, Geraldine, Soaphead, etc.

Most books have a likable character you can "identify with"—put yourself in her shoes. That's Claudia. Each season begins with Claudia telling us what that season means to her (as a grown woman looking back) and how it affected Pecola's situation in her last year. You might think that since this is Pecola's story—it's her tragedy—she should be the one who tells it. Why doesn't TM have Pecola tell her own story? If Pecola had enough self-awareness to tell her story, there would be no story. She would understand that judging herself by white standards of beauty is something she has to fight her way through, not something you accept with your whole heart and being. Claudia and Frieda have been subjected to the same impossible standard of beauty as Pecola; they're affected by it, but they fight it.

What about Cholly, Pecola's father? In TM's view, Cholly's rape of his daughter was a twisted attempt at love, distorted by violence and expressed in violence. (She's too easy on him.)

. . . that ends what I would call The Idealized Version of *The Bluest Eye.*

If you'd like an alternative view of *The Bluest Eye* (or if you just enjoy peeking into the minds of smart people) check out Barbara Christian and Michael Awkward.

≈≈≈≈≈≈≈≈≈≈≈≈≈≈≈≈≈≈≈≈≈≈≈≈≈≈≈≈≈≈≈≈≈≈≈≈≈≈≈≈≈≈≈

The best take on the form of *The Bluest Eye* is Barbara Christian's. My "Idealized Version" of the novel leans all over her essay. It's a brilliant piece, generous, even beautiful (in the sense that it finds the Idealized Design of *The Bluest Eye* and *Sula*). Christian has not only put her finger on the Idealized Design of the novel, she's taken everything that might be considered flawed in the book and turned it into a virtue. (Hell, if she did that for me, I'd put her down as coauthor!)

Some critics felt that *The Bluest Eye* mirrored what early black scholar W.E.B. Du Bois called the "double-consciousness of the Afro-American." (A black person living in a white country has to learn to think with "two minds"—his own and the white man's—if he has any interest in survival.) The most thorough exploration of that theory is by Michael Awkward. Awkward isn't wishy washy. He lays it right out there:

- "An exploration of Du Boissian double-consciousness is at the center of the narrative events depicted in *The Bluest Eye.*"
- "Pecola's splitting into two voices corresponds directly to the two-voiced narration of *The Bluest Eye.*"
- "Morrison's novel has been narrated by two distinct voices: by Claudia and by an omniscient presence."

≈≈≈≈≈≈≈≈≈≈≈≈≈≈≈≈≈≈≈≈≈≈≈≈≈≈≈≈≈≈≈≈≈≈≈≈≈≈≈≈≈≈≈

## WHAT'D THE CRITICS SAY ABOUT THE BOOK?

For the most part, if they didn't like it, they didn't bother to review it. Most of the reviews had something good to say and something not so good, but almost all of them ended up with more plusses than minuses.

She reveals herself, when she shucks the fuzziness born of flights of poetic imagery, as a writer of considerable power and tenderness, someone who can cast back to the living, bleeding heart of childhood and capture it on paper. But Miss Morrison has gotten lost in her construction.

—Haskel Frankel, *New York Times Book Review*

*The Bluest Eye* is not flawless. Miss Morrison's touching and disturbing picture of the doomed youth of her race is marred by an occasional error of fact or judgment. She places the story in a frame of the bland white words of a conventional school "reader"—surely an unnecessary and unsubtle irony. She permits herself an occasional false or bombastic line. . . . None of this matters, though, beside her real and greatly promising achievement: to write truly (and sometimes very beautifully) of every generation of blacks. . . .

—L. E. Sissman, *New Yorker*

She got some hard compliments:

[Morrison had the courage to write about] an aspect of the Black experience that most of us would rather forget, our hatred of ourselves.

—Liz Gant, *Black World*

And she got at least one review to die for:

[She writes] a prose so precise, so faithful to speech and so charged with pain and wonder that the novel becomes pure poetry.

—John Leonard, *New York Times*

## WHAT DID TONI MORRISON HAVE TO SAY?

### Conversation with Jane Bakerman

**Morrison:** I thought in The Bluest Eye that I was writing about beauty, miracles, and self-images, about the way in which people can hurt each other about whether or not one is beautiful.

### Conversation with Anna Koenen

**Koenen:** You seem . . . suspicious of romantic feelings . . . like when you say in The Bluest Eye that the idea of romantic love is one of the most dangerous ideas which exist.

**Morrison:** [W]ho wants it, romantic love? The women who would want it are precisely the kind of women I would never like to be. In other words, it's a complicity between master and servant.

(Don't be shy, baby—jump in her face!)

### Conversation with Robert Stepto

**Morrison:** [Morrison tells Stepto that, much to her surprise, she wrote Cholly straight through. But] when I got to Pauline, whom I knew so well, I could not do it. . . . I didn't know what to write or how. And I sort of copped out anyway in the book because I used two voices, hers and the author's. There were certain things she couldn't know and I had to come in. And then there were certain things the author would say that I wanted in her language—so that there were the two things, two voices, which I had regarded . . . as a way in which to do something second-best. I couldn't do it straight out the way I did every other section.

When Toni Morrison said THAT, I knew it was time to talk about the negative, downright amateurish, aspects of *The Bluest Eye* . . . and to do it frankly and openly, without pulling any punches.

I gave you the Idealized Version of *The Bluest Eye*.

Now I'd like to tell you how, in my opinion, *The Bluest Eye* measured up to that Ideal. First, the short version.

## DOING 99 YEARS TO LIFE

*The Bluest Eye* is built around a great idea; it has an unforgettable image at its center; it has a theme of life-and-death importance to half of the people in the world (and great moral importance to the other half if they can get out from under their denial long enough to face it); it has a beautiful cyclic design; fairly (but not enormously) interesting characters; some of the finest line-to-line writing you'll ever see in your life—and an author who seems determined to do everything in her power to undermine her own book. If you could be arrested for sabotaging a novel with great potential, Toni Morrison would be doing 99 years to life for the ways she mangled *The Bluest Eye*.

But it was her first book. As a writer, she was just a kid. She made an amateur's mistakes because she was an amateur. Unfortunately, as far as I know, neither Morrison nor her fans have ever dealt with that openly and honestly. Toni Morrison has written three of the best novels in the world. Her best work is breathtaking. But she did not come into the world a fully formed novelist (who does?), and it is an insult to her best work to pretend that she did. Even worse, it plays a dirty trick on the thousands of writers who imitate everything she does, including her mistakes and amateurisms.

Please don't take my word for that (or for anything else). If what I say makes sense to you, go with it. If it doesn't, don't.

Specific examples will follow this important Public Service Announcement:

*T*HE *"IN MY OPINION" SIDEBAR* ≈≈≈≈≈≈≈≈≈≈≈≈≈≈≈≈≈≈≈≈≈≈

Instead of murdering every phrase I write by prefacing it with "in my opinion," I'm going to ask you to understand that it applies to everything I say here—and to almost everything I say in this book.

It's not the Truth. It's not a Fact. It's my opinion.

But don't, even in your mind, preface it with the word "only" and "humblify" the living juice out of it, because there's nothing humble or "only" about it. I work conscientiously and passionately to form the best, truest, most useful opinions that I can come up with. I'm just not dumb enough to think they're the Truth.

≈≈≈≈≈≈≈≈≈≈≈≈≈≈≈≈≈≈≈≈≈≈≈≈≈≈≈≈≈≈≈≈≈≈≈≈≈≈≈≈≈≈≈≈≈≈

## HOW DID TM SABOTAGE HER OWN NOVEL?

Two of Toni Morrison's goals—the sense of intimacy (you're sitting over coffee listening to a real person tell you the story) and writing that has the heartbeat of spoken language—work in such close combination that it's often impossible to distinguish one from the other. A fair amount of the time, TM did pull off that combination of intimacy and the illusion of spoken language beautifully. When it was good, it was so good that when the flow was interrupted, you felt like you'd stepped into a hole.

There were two ways in which Toni Morrison repeatedly destroyed the illusion of real people talking intimately in *The Bluest Eye:*

- Using the wrong-sized language
- Using an over-complicated assortment of narrators (to tell the story)

USING THE WRONG-SIZED LANGUAGE: If any one aspect of the writing killed the illusion of real people in intimate conversation, it is the fact that so much of the book is told in language that the characters in the novel (including the person narrating the novel at that particular time) would never use. If your story is about very young people or about people who use "neighborhood" language, if you want me to have the feeling that a real person is telling me a story over coffee, the person telling me the story should talk in the language of the neighborhood or of young people. But if Shakespeare's little sister tells me the story, I will no doubt hear some beautiful language, but it will be at the expense of any sense of real people from the neighborhood letting me in on a little graveyard information.

What hurts most is when Toni Morrison has worked hard to build these wonderful effects and combine them into something as successful and moving as the night the three girls lay in bed after Pecola had her first period. Then suddenly this finishing school language lady that is supposed to be grown-up Claudia pipes up, but regardless of who or what she is, her high-falutin' words destroy every illusion of reality, intimacy, and real people engaged in real talk.

There are sections in *The Bluest Eye* where, to be perfectly blunt about it, the language is so tight-assed that I can't imagine it spoken by anyone. The most schoolmarmish line in the book (if not the Universe) was given to poor little Claudia. Claudia, an interesting and intense eight-year-old child, is dying to rip a plastic blond doll apart, "to see of what it was made." Some lady with her blue hair in a bun and her eyeglasses on a chain may have said that once, but I doubt that any eight-year-old in the universe has ever used those words. Toni Morrison, with patience and skill, manages to create this fascinating, headstrong child doing something so real and meaningful that we are in there with her, when the narrator drops a line that's more out of place than a fart in church: *To see of what it was made.* BAM—just that quick, we're jolted out of the reality of the novel. The line mocks the child that was supposed to have spoken or thought it . . . and brings to mind a fine line we once read: "We substituted good grammar for intellect . . ."

In TM's defense, *The Bluest Eye* was her first novel. Contrast that with *Beloved,* which is told in language that is never fancier than the characters it describes, yet manages to cover a range of emotions most of us can barely imagine.

USING AN OVER-COMPLICATED ASSORTMENT OF NARRATORS TO TELL THE STORY: I took Toni Morrison's notion of an African-American novel so seriously that I was determined to be her ideal reader. Picture me sitting across the table from the storyteller (I think it's young Claudia) just as TM wants me to, ready for coffee, intimacy, just dyin' for some nasty Graveyard Information—then the person I'm sitting across from switches from young Claudia to old Claudia (I think it's old Claudia but since I don't know a single thing about her [how old is she? where is she? what's she look like? is she a school teacher? housewife? hooker? or just some fleshless mouthpiece TM invented to tell the story?], I wouldn't bet on it). Old Claudia or whoever says a few words, then the person sitting intimately across the table from me switches to Pecola, Pecola becomes Polly who turns into Cholly, Cholly gives way to Soaphead, and Soaphead evaporates to make room at the table for this Supermama who seems to be to a cross between God, Freud, and Toni Morrison! (That was one crowded-assed table!) As we've already noted, some fine critics say that TM told *The Bluest Eye* from two viewpoints (DuBois's "double consciousness"), but *The Bluest Eye* didn't have two consciousnesses—it had a dozen. The sheer number of narrators would have pretty much squelched the intimacy TM sought—but just in case they hadn't, TM added the Kiss of Death: the Cosmic Narrator.

The Cosmic Narrator (the Godlike Dude that knows everything about everybody and can zoom through time and space, in one person's head and out the other) massacres the illusion of Real People rapping over a cup of coffee, and absolutely slaughters reality: I was sitting there having coffee with this Cosmic Narrator who was telling me the thoughts of 27 people at the same time!?

## "STACKING" NARRATORS

Stacking narrators is not a technical term but comes close to describing what the narrative structure of *The Bluest Eye* feels like to me: I can't take credit for this first one because TM mentioned it in an interview: She started out with one narrator, Pecola; then she realized that if Pecola could see a situation clearly enough to describe it effectively, she wouldn't have been "blindsided" by her need for blue eyes. So TM adds (horizontally = more characters spread along the floor of the story for example, the more "normal" Claudia who we identify with and contrast to Pecola. Then TM adds a couple more—say Cholly and Pauline—then decides (TM didn't say this, it's merely my "it feels as if") that these people aren't smart enough to tell all the ramifications of the story, so she invents Claudia The-Grownup, who talks like a grammar book. The point is simple but important: unless you're importing a character who is different than everyone in the story precisely because he IS different and you intend to use his differentness as a major part of the story—Starman from Planet X suddenly finds himself in Detroit?—it's going to be like Porgy talking like Shakespeare.

Another situation that I feel makes characters look dumb and makes a story unrealistic is when a narrator knows more about the characters than they know about themselves—like when TM's narrator, referring to Pauline Breedlove, says:

> [S]he liked, most of all to arrange things. . . . To line things up in rows. . . . She missed without knowing that she missed—paints and crayons.

Sure, the writing is pretty—but a writer who knows more about her characters than they know about themselves (in MY opinion) is doing some serious cheating. What is this "cheating" stuff again? It's the narrator "knowing" (presuming to know) what she can't possibly know.

It's often claimed that TM's narration scheme isn't significantly different than Faulkner's. See the sidebar next door for my take on that interesting question.

Enough with the stinkin' narrators. Let's see if we can find another excellent way to sabotage our novel.

## An Awesome Way to Sabotage Your Novel, Dude

One of the best ways to guarantee that most people will NOT finish reading your novel is to digress a lot. And make the digressions lengthy. Long digressions bring your story to a screeching halt.

Toni Morrison digresses a lot. That's surely one of the main reasons that even people who love her work usually leave a couple of her novels half-read. I could stand on a tall soapbox and continue to lecture TM for sabotaging an almost-fine novel with all those digressions, but I promised you the truth.

Here's the truth: in *The Bluest Eye,* TM's digressions contain some of the most beautiful writing in the book (if not the universe). So even if her digressions drive you up the wall, register your complaints with the proper authorities, then do your best to get over it and enjoy them for all they're worth! I say it now and I'll say it again: When she's on her game, it is not possible to overestimate the writing of Toni Morrison. It took her awhile to become a great novelist, but Toni

### Are TM's Multiple Narrators in *The Bluest Eye* Really Any Different Than Faulkner's?

*Different* is starting at the wrong end of the scale. As far as I can tell they have nothing in common other than the fact that they're both "multiple." Faulkner's most famous narrative experiments were *The Sound and the Fury* and *As I Lay Dying. Sound and the Fury* is divided into four sections. The first three sections are each told from the point of view of one individual (Benjy, Quentin, Jason); they never exceed the limits of what that person thinks, sees, and knows first-hand. The fourth section has an omniscient narrator, primarily external, like a movie camera: nothing cosmic or fancy about it.

*As I Lay Dying* has 59 sections, narrated by 18 different people. But each section is exactly, only, and entirely what that one person sees and thinks: *I* see this, *I* think that—no Cosmic Narrators. No "cheating."

Morrison's handling of multiple narrators in *Beloved* was again different than Faulkner's, but if anything, TM's was better. She didn't do any one thing that was as in-your-face-brilliant as Faulker's four narrators *(Sound & Fury)* taking us, little by little, from chaos to clarity. But Faulkner's shifts from one narrator to another felt so well planned and so consciously arranged that they seemed artificial compared to TM's soft, unpredictable shifts that seemed so natural that they must have happened on their own. Morrison's handling of multiple narrators in *Beloved* was as good as anybody's, ever . . . so sweet and gentle the shifts were almost invisible.

Morrison was a great writer from the minute she hit the scene. (She had to be to get away with all those digressions!)

Despite her writing skills, I don't think there's any doubt: Morrison's digressions did hurt her books and limit her readers. I am not suggesting that's bad news for her; it's them I feel sorry for. (They'll miss, without knowing that they missed, some of the best writing they've never read.)

I honestly think that most fairly open-minded people will understand and agree with my explanation of the ways in which Toni Morrison sabotaged *The Bluest Eye.* But I'd be surprised if many of you agreed with what I'm about to say when you first hear it. After it's had time to roll around inside your head awhile, quite a few of you will agree with me.

Two days after I wrote "They'll miss, without knowing . . . ," several things hit me at once (1) In a sense, the most (or only) important question isn't How good is the book? It's How good does it make me when I read it? (2) This was provoked by my thinking back on my "They'll miss, without knowing . . ." line, loving the wit and truth in that context and hoping that it would not hurt TM's feelings even a tiny bit, but that she would realize what I had realized: that line—and this entire book—aren't mine, it/they are ours. Just as I (and every reader) change her books when I read them, her books change me—and what I write about them. (3) I had never thought of my book as being in any way a manifestation of the "reader involvement" Toni Morrison sought, but when I saw so clearly that "my" line was made almost entirely of "her" words . . . it seemed to me that what I had considered "my" book was in fact "our" book (so if you don't like it, Chloe, you have no one to blame but yourself!).

## WAS IT AN ACT OF GRATUITOUS VIOLENCE THAT HURT THE STORY?

Cholly's rape of Pecola struck me as pure gratuitous violence. It not only didn't add to the story, it subtracted from it. First of all, the rape scene came out of nowhere. A sweet little scene, then BAM—the rape. TM was too lady-like to really tell us about the rape, so BAM—it stopped as abruptly as it started. Whatever else we may have thought of Cholly up to that time, raping his daughter did not (to me) seem like something he'd do. The only thing that made me stop and do a Yes-But, was the fact that TM had "announced" early in the novel that Cholly had raped Pecola. But an Announcement doesn't preclude the need for motivation . . . or for a character to act in character. Also it's strongly implied that Pecola's rape by her father somehow caused (or strongly contributed to) her "need" for blue eyes. I don't buy it. Her father rapes her; therefore she wants blue eyes? Why?—so that she'll be so foxy that every rapist in the neighborhood will want her? (*Author's Note:* Here, my editor Manie Barron, wrote, "Couldn't Pecola also be thinking that white women don't get raped?" It would be comforting to believe that Manie-the-Individual thought of that, instead of considering it the kind of thing that non-black readers miss.)

The rape was an oversized event that drew attention to itself at the expense of the tiny, almost gentle breakdown of a little girl. Worse yet, the rape diverted atten-

> ## . . . But She Pulled Off a Small Miracle
>
> The fact that Toni Morrison didn't pull off everything she tried is exactly what you'd expect in a first novel. But what she did accomplish in *The Bluest Eye* is so huge and subtle that it seems impossible: if you traced Pecola's self-hatred and the reactions of the young girls in the disgusting pick-the-prettiest-girl-out-of-the-picture experiment and everything in between, the root cause would surely be white racism. I think we all know that. I also think it's virtually impossible to prove.
>
> But somehow TM proved it in *The Bluest Eye.* Toni Morrison drives the "art for art's sake" people crazy with her insistence that "ALL GOOD ART IS POLITICAL." On the surface, *The Bluest Eye* might not strike you as a political novel, but *The Bluest Eye* is as political as it gets.
>
> In what sense? No child just wakes up one day with a need for blue eyes. Pecola wants blue eyes because three hundred years of history have hammered home the message that everything about her is less beautiful and less worthy than the dominant white society's Barbie doll notion of beauty.
>
> That is a radical political statement.

tion away from the gruesome truth at the center of *The Bluest Eye:* white society's campaign to impose its One Standard of Beauty on everyone, including people of color, carried to its logical conclusion, ends up at Pecola's self-hate. (See Sidebar) That self-hate doesn't need an "extra" event like rape; it comes to fruition all by its ugly self.

## NEGATIVE VIEW OR A TRAGIC VIEW?

Despite the beautiful writing, *The Bluest Eye* is a misery-filled novel: TM's characters are a miserable bunch; they bring misery on each other and misery on themselves. Morrison (who's given more interviews than the Dallas Cowboys) says she has "a tragic view" of the world, but it isn't; it's a negative view. The defining characteristic of the Tragic View is a belief that the universe is beautiful, logical, orderly, and just: you always get what you deserve (even if you have to give it to yourself). In Morrison's view, ugly stays ugly and nobody is dumb enough to expect justice. When you witness a tragic drama, everything ties together so beautifully that you experience what Aristotle called a catharsis (a sort of intellectual o-r-g-a-s-m). In her list of goals for an African-American novel, Toni Morrison clearly states her strong opposition to fiction that ties everything into a neat package and gives us a sense of satisfaction.

In *The Bluest Eye,* this beautiful, strong, writerwoman expresses one of the most negative views of human beings I've ever seen. But she loves the hell out of Nature (a literary version of a person who loves dogs and trees but ain't none too fond of people). Morrison writes about us like we're a bunch of rectumheads and talks about us like we're her own children. But, my God, she does it with such beautiful language . . .

If Toni Morrison had never written anything other than this little lovesong about that prick Cholly, I would call her one of the finest writers in the country. Morrison's language is so beautiful and her wisdom runs so deep that you can't even hate Cholly, the creep who rapes his daughter. She understands us even when we don't understand ourselves . . .

> The pieces of Cholly's life could become coherent only in the head of a musician. Only those who talk their talk through the gold of curved metal, or in the touch of black-and-white rectangles could give true form to his life. Only they would know how to connect the heart of a red watermelon . . . to the flashlight on his behind to the fists of money to the lemonade in a Mason jar to a man called Blue and come up with all that it meant in joy, in pain, in anger, in love, and give it its final and pervading ache of freedom.

But to do it, she had to bring in one of those I-know-more-about-you-than-you-know-about-yourself narrators . . . (It's hard to complain with any conviction when you have writing like Morrison's staring you in the face: Shakespeare's little sister, for sure.)

Within weeks after her latest novel *Paradise* came out, Toni Morrison appeared on both the "Charlie Rose Show" and "60 Minutes," where she was interviewed by Ed Bradley. On both shows she said things that I've been thinking about ever since. Toni Morrison talked almost affectionately about the way she had to repress the urge to edit her earlier books. I think it would be wonderful if she DID rewrite one of them. (She's broken every other rule in the book. What's so sacred about that one?) If she does decide to do it and has any interest in outside opinions, I'd love to see her rewrite *The Bluest Eye*. It may be the most flawed of her books, but it has a greater moral presence and a more urgent life-and-death problem at its center than any of her novels except *Beloved*. A few more reasons to do it?

1. So that aspiring writers could "go to school on it."
2. So that experienced writers could "go to school on it."
3. It would give literary criticism the possibility of being (for once) constructive.
4. It would not replace the original version; it would stand on its own.
5. It would be required reading in every writing class.
6. . . . And it would surely be a best-seller.

*I thought of Sula as a cracked mirror, fragments and pieces we have to see independently and put together.*
　　—Toni Morrison to Thomas LeClair


*Let us do evil, that good may come.*
　　—Romans 3:8


# SULA
## *(1973)*


As you may remember from Toni Morrison's bio, her second novel, *Sula,* was created out of the feeling that black women related to each other in a different way than white women. Perceptive critics like Barbara Christian and Robert Stepto felt that *Sula* was a natural progression from *The Bluest Eye.* Toni Morrison lent credence to that notion when she mentioned that it was natural to wonder what little girls like Claudia and Frieda are like when they grow up.

*Sula* has a large cast of the wackiest, weirdest, most wonderful characters you've ever seen, especially the supporting cast. We'll meet them before we do the main story. I say main story because each character has a story of her own—including the neighborhood!

---

### A Few Major Minor Characters

**The Bottom** = Only TM could make a neighborhood's nickname into one of the characters. It's really very simple: The black neighborhood, called The Bottom, is really on top because the white guys . . . on second thought, maybe you had to be there.

**Shadrack** = He came back from World War I, shell-shocked— "permanently astonished"—did time in a Vet's hospital, and invented National Suicide Day.

*continued*

---

## A Few Major Minor Characters

**One-Legged Eva** = Sula's grandmother: "Fewer than nine people in town remembered when Eva had two legs, and her oldest child, Hannah, was not one of them."

**Hannah** = Eva's daughter; Sula's mother: She'd have sex with anyone, but she was very choosy about where she slept.

**The Three Deweys** = "One-Legged Eva took in stray children and named them by the way they looked: She looked the first child over and said, 'Well look at Dewey. My my mymymy.' Later that year she sent for a kid who kept falling off the porch . . . and named him Dewey, too. 'But Miss Eva, you calls the other one Dewey.' "

(. . . and so on; it's one of the wackiest things I've ever read; damn, I love it!)

**Tar Baby** = One-Legged Eva's tenant. The neighborhood said he was half white, but "Eva said he was all white. That she knew blood when she saw it, and he didn't have none." He had pale white skin and yellow hair so, naturally, she called him Tar Baby.

**Ajax** = A "twenty-one-year-old pool haunt of sinister beauty" envied by men of all shoe sizes for his "magnificently foul mouth."

I'm sure you get the idea. For my tastes, Part One of *Sula* may be the best written book I've ever read. Lord, the woman can sing!

## A QUICK LOOK AT THE STORY

*Sula,* set in the "squinchy little town" of Medallion, Ohio, between 1919 and 1965, is the story of two black women, Nel Wright and Sula Peace. They met at the age of twelve, both "wishbone thin and easy-assed," both only children, both friendless except for each other, and both determined to explore everything in the world.

On the way home from school, four white boys knock Nel around. Nel avoids them. One day, Sula insists they walk past the boys' hangout. When the boys approach, itching for fun, Sula takes out a knife and cuts off the tip of her finger. She looks at the boys and says quietly, "If I can do that to myself, what you suppose I'll do to you?"

One day around the time that Sula hears her mother say, "I love Sula. I just don't like her," Nel and Sula are playing down by the river. Sula is swinging a young boy around in a circle, when suddenly, he slips from her hands and swoops into the water:

> The water darkened and closed quickly over the place where Chicken Little sank. The pressure of his hand and tight little fingers was still in Sula's palms as she stood looking at the closed place in the water.

The girls know they're responsible for the boy's drowning, but they don't tell anyone. At the boy's funeral, Nel stands expressionless while Sula cries uncontrollably. Standing together a safe distance from the boy's grave, they hold hands in a tight clench, then relax slowly, and walk home.

A few years later, Sula leaves town in search of the "experimental life." Nel marries a dude named Jude and settles into a life of serious housewifing.

Ten years later—1937, the year Medallion had a plague of robins—Sula comes back to town. At Eva's house there are four dead robins on the sidewalk. Sula pushes them with her toe into the grass. When One-Legged Eva sees Sula at the door, she says:

> "I might have knowed them birds meant something. Where's your coat?"
> After a little small talk, Sula says, "Don't you say hello to nobody when you ain't seen them for ten years?"

> "If folks let somebody know where they is and when they coming, then other folks can get ready for them."

About a minute after she finishes unpacking, Sula steals Nel's husband and puts Eva in an old folks' home. In no time at all, everyone in town hates her. ("She came to their church suppers without underwear.") The townspeople begin to define their lives in contrast to hers; they begin to "cherish their husbands and wives, protect their children, repair their homes and in general band together against the devil in their midst."

Sula dies young out of sheer orneriness, but she dies beautifully. (For me, her dying was the only thing she did in Part Two of the novel that measured up to TM's attempt to "sell" her as a character who lived an "experimental life.")

> A crease of fear touched her breast, for any second there was sure to be a violent explosion in her brain, a gasping for breath. Then she realized, or rather she sensed, that there was not going to be any pain. She was not breathing because she didn't have to. Her body did not need oxygen. She was dead.
>
> Sula felt her face smiling. "Well, I'll be damned," she thought, "it didn't even hurt. Wait'll I tell Nel."

Years after she dies, in a flash of insight that puts everything in perspective, Nel sees that her friendship with Sula transcends everything. As the book ends, Nel hears Sula's voice blowing through the treetops near the old cemetery and she realizes that all the years she thought she was missing her husband, she was actually missing her friend:

> And the loss pressed down on her chest and came up in her throat. "We was girls together," she said as though explaining something.
>
> "O Lord, Sula," she cried, "girl, girl girlgirlgirl."

## WHAT DID THE CRITICS SAY?

Toni Morrison's *Sula* is a rebel idea, both for her creator and for Morrison's audience. To read *Sula* is to encounter a sentimental education so sharply discontinuous from the dominant traditions of Afro-American literature in the way that it compels and/or deadlocks the response that the novel . . . is, to my mind, the single most important erruption of black women's writing in our era.

—Hortense J. Spillers, *Feminist Studies*

The heroine, Sula, grows up in a household pulsing with larger-than-life people and activity, presided over by her powerful and probably sorceress grandmother. Her gentle mother is devoted almost wholly to the practice and pleasures of sensuality. But her cherished friend, Nel, the local goody-goody, plays perfect counterpoint to Sula's intense, life-grabbing insistence on freedom.

When the rage gets directed at its characters as intensely as it does against the conditions that formed them, the bitterness sometimes takes over. One scene, in which the child Nel witnesses her majestic, usually holier-than-thou mother cringing before a brutal, repulsive, white train conductor, is close to devastating: the mother is depicted with an unsparing irony, unforgiven.

As the author of frequent criticism and social commentary, Morrison has shown herself someone of considerable strength and skill in confronting current realities, and it's frustrating that the qualities which distinguish her novels are not combined with the stinging immediacy, the urgency, of her nonfiction.

—Sarah Blackburn, *New York Times Book Review*

In Morrison's narrative of a unique female friendship, Sula and Nel initially discover their own essences and begin to grow through their reciprocal connection; each girl seems to have, both materially and metaphysically, what the other lacks.

—Roberta Rubenstein, *Boundaries of the Self: Gender, Culture, Fiction*

The feeling I get from this, however, is not so much that of the familiar literary viewpoint of moral complexity as that of a calm sardonic irony over the impossibility of ever sorting out the good from the bad. This feeling gives *Sula* a portentousness that makes it perhaps an inadvertent prophet, whose prophecy is that all our old assumptions about morality are disintegrating before a peculiarly black assault against them. It is as if Morrison, and other young black writers with her, are saying, like Sula, *If we can do this to ourselves, you can imagine what we can do to you.*

—Jerry H. Bryant, *Nation*

## In Her Own Words . . .

### Rappin' with Robert Stepto

**Morrison:** . . . one can never really define good and evil. Sometimes good looks like evil; sometimes evil looks like good—you never really know what it is. It depends on what uses you put it to. Evil is as useful as good is. . . .

. . . if they had been one person, I suppose they would have been a rather marvelous person. But each one lacked something that the other had.

Sula did the one terrible thing for black people which was to put her grandmother in an old folks' home, which was outrageous, you know.

### Rappin' with Jane Bakerman

**Bakerman:** One of the great attractions of *Sula*, especially for female readers, is its examination of a friendship between two women.

### Rappin' with Anna Koenen

**Koenen:** Why is it that the relationships between men and women in your novels fall apart?

**Morrison:** I think that is because my mode of writing is sublimely didactic in the sense that I can only warn by taking something away. What I really wanted to say about the friendship between Nel and Sula was that if you really do have a friend, a real other, another person that complements your life, you should stay with him or her.

**Me:** Let's resurrect that quote with which we opened the intro to the novels . . .

---

**Didactic**

intended to make a moral point; designed to give moral instruction; preachy

Most writers want to stab you if you call them didactic, but TM, who does everything in her own personal way, refers to her own writing as "sublimely didactic." She feels there's no point in writing if it doesn't teach a moral lesson. The only trouble with that is, sometimes you have to force your characters to go where they don't want to go in order to prove your point . . .

---

≈≈≈≈≈≈≈≈≈≈≈≈≈≈≈≈≈≈≈≈≈≈≈≈≈≈≈≈≈≈≈≈≈≈≈≈≈≈≈≈≈≈≈≈≈≈≈

Forget about what I say in an interview

—it might be anything—

but trust the tale and start with that.

≈≈≈≈≈≈≈≈≈≈≈≈≈≈≈≈≈≈≈≈≈≈≈≈≈≈≈≈≈≈≈≈≈≈≈≈≈≈≈≈≈≈≈≈≈≈≈

If I forget what TM says in her interviews and simply "trust the tale," I have a few serious questions—for starters:

## WHY ARE WE LYING TO OURSELVES ABOUT SULA'S CHARACTER?

If you didn't have Toni Morrison hanging off the side of her novel "explaining" that although Sula appears to be a self-absorbed brat, she is, in fact, the standard-bearer of some super new morality where good looks like evil and evil looks like—gimme a break!—Sula is brutal.

(Intelligent people like to think that intelligence is the most important quality in the world, utterly indispensable in any situation. That's why smart people can be clueless when it comes to morality. They can't believe that after several thousand years of philosophy, science, technology, and every imaginable kind of intellectual and cultural cross-dressing, morality still boils down to this: Treat other people the way you'd like them to treat you.)

If you want to be treated like Sula treated Nel, I feel sorry for your sorry ass.

## WAS PART TWO A NOVEL OR A THEORY ABOUT A NOVEL?

To me, *Sula* is two separate books. Part One is the best-written half of a book I've ever read. Part Two almost isn't a novel. It's as if the main characters have left town and in their place are sociological descriptions of why they are the way they are:

> The first experience [her mother saying that she loved Sula but didn't like her] taught her that there was no other that you could count on; the second [Chicken Little's drowning] that there was no self to count on either. She had no center, no speck around which to grow.

Then TM tells us that Sula should have been an artist, but that nobody ever gave her the blah blah blah. TM, baby, even in fiction—especially in fiction—just saying it doesn't make it so. Where's the evidence? Sula went away for ten years' worth of "experimental life"—she could have painted. (Not to mention the fact that you already used that coulda-been-an-artist stuff on Pauline in *The Bluest Eye*.) Sula went away for ten years to put together an interesting self . . . and when she came back, she was less interesting than her mother and nowhere near as interesting as old One-Legged Eva. If you wanted to tell me that Eva challenged conventional morality, I could certainly get next to that.

## DID SHE **tell** WHEN SHE SHOULD'VE **shown**?

One of the oddest aspects of Part Two of *Sula* is TM's choice of which scenes and events to "dramatize" and which to skip. She skips the ten years of Sula's absence . . . interesting strategy. Then she skips right from Jude saying Sula fascinates the mind but doesn't attract the body to Jude and Sula doing something ostensibly sexual (arf arf). That could have been real interesting, but since she'd just skipped across ten years, it felt like the author was losing interest in her own material. The "poetic" description of sex that fills the next several pages doesn't have anything to do with any kind of sex I've ever had. Toni Morrison, who can sum up a lifetime in fifty words, spent a dozen pages on abstract hogwash that pretended to be about sex.

> Around the time that TM wrote *Sula*, Jerzy Kosinski wrote a novel that, like *Sula*, was lauded for its "sensitivity." The sensitive young hero of Kosinski's sensitive novel fed razor blades (or was it broken glass?) to an old couple.

And when I read in reviews that Sula's badness made the townspeople good, I thought, "Those people must be sensitive readers to pick up something that subtle." Then when I read the book, I had to laugh: TM doesn't show us that Sula's badness makes the townspeople good, she just announces it. The writer has a nice theory, but nothing happens before my eyes to convince me that Sula's badness makes people good.

## HOW DO I JUDGE THEE— REAL OR SURREAL?

Part One of *Sula* is surrealistic, fantastic; Part Two is much more realistic. That poses a problem for the reader: how do I judge the events and people in Part Two? Do I judge them by the wonderful, whacko, surrealistic standards of Part One (where a woman can "sell" her leg, make three individu-

### Telling vs. Showing

In a sense, a story writer has only two options: she can either tell you what happened, or she can show you (dramatize or present in a scene). Virtually every story (novel, movie, play) has a bit of both. The usual approach is, tell the least important things, and show the most important ones.

### To Show or Not

Take the New Testament, for example: we are told in a sentence or two that Jesus spent the years between ages 12 and 30 preparing himself for the last three years of his life. Then we are shown those last three years in great detail. The more extraordinary the events, the more important it is to show them. If the authors of the New Testament had described Jesus' more-or-less average pre-age-30 life in great detail, then polished off his last three years in a sentence or two, there'd be no such religion as Christianity.

als identical by calling them Dewey, and burn her son to death for his own good), or do I judge them by regular old everyday 9-to-5 standards where putting your grandmother in an old folks' home is the top Evil?

Toni Morrison puts together words better than any writer I know but sometimes, when I try to make sense of her ideas, I end up shaking my head in disbelief. How can anyone write a book in which a woman burns her son to death, a girl casually watches her mother burn to death, two girls responsible for a child's drowning don't mention it to his parents, and a lady's best friend steals her husband—after all that and more—and then say the worst thing you could possibly do—the ONE terrible thing—is to put your grandmother in an old folks' home. Toni Morrison is not only a great writer, she's REALLY smart. But that's one of the most bizarre statements I've ever heard.

My editor's note (printed below) cleared up any confusion I had about nursing homes. I left most of my mouth on the page so that others could see what NOT to say. Sorry if I hurt anyone's feelings.

> ### Sula, the Role Model
>
> Not long after reading the article that I raved about in the chapter on *The Bluest Eye* ("The Contemporary Fables of Toni Morrison"), I decided that it would be obscene to enjoy a piece of writing that much and not tell the author, so I got Barbara Christian's phone number from information and I called and left a most enthusiastic message. She phoned me back a couple days later and left me a most enthusiastic message. We finally connected and, not too surprisingly, we talked about Toni Morrison. Barbara Christian (still excited twenty-five years after the fact) described how she and all the other brainy young black women at the university knew that Toni Morrison was writing a book about how serious, strong, unconventional black women should live their lives their way and not be deterred by friends, family, or men. Of course, the book was *Sula*, and while I have obviously given my irreverence free rein, Sula-as-Role-Model means too much to people I respect for me to simply dismiss her and let my mind close. If *Sula* means a great deal to people I care about, then *Sula* means a great deal to me. (Barbara Christian doesn't know it yet, but I learned that from her.)

Ron—You talk about the unbelievability of Toni Morrison's responses to Eva's incarceration? However, if you look at her desire to write African-

American novels, it is believable. Blacks WOULD say putting Eva away was the worst thing in the book. So TM's still following her dictum on writing. What do you think?

—Manie Barron, Editor

I think that the word incarceration tells me exactly how you feel about nursing homes.

## A FEW THINGS TO NOTE

- TM ventures two off-the-wall but very interesting theories:
  - White people try to obliterate Evil; black people accept Evil as part of life.
  - The presence of Evil can cause Good. (I was so surprised to find a quote from the Bible expressing the same idea that I just had to open this chapter with it.
- The "Doubling" strategies we discussed in *The Bluest Eye* are at the heart of *Sula:*
  - Nel and Sula go from a Similar Pair to a Contrasting Pair.
  - Sula and Nel can/should also be looked at as incomplete halves of a whole. As TM said, if you put them together, they'd make a great person.
- "Funny" isn't a term you normally associate with Toni Morrison's writing, but Part One of *Sula* is absolutely hilarious—which was all the more surprising to me because all of the reviews I read focused only on the grimness.
- I was surprised that quite a few people didn't find *Sula* one bit funny. Many people, in fact, found it downright horrible and brutal. For reasons I can't quite identify, *Sula,* more than any book I know, horrified some people and tickled the hell out of others. For me, the humor was a response that presumed that the truly bizarre people—especially One-Legged Eva—were not realistic characters. They were surreal; metaphors, not mere people.
- There was one long section in Part One that I must admit I hated: the humiliation of Nel's mother, Helene. There was a similar but worse scene

in *Bluest Eye* where Cholly went looking for his father and shit all over himself. Any honest accounting of TM's recurring "themes" would have to include Shit and Humiliation.

- It may be cheating to look ahead to TM's next novel, which is largely about the importance of names, but it seemed remarkably insensitive for Toni Morrison to name the little kid who drowned "Chicken Little," reducing him to a nitwit in a cartoon.
- One of the things that bothered me most—and it seems to be a pattern in TM's novels—is that she seems to force her characters into whatever ending she had originally outlined for the novel, even though the characters may have taken the novel in a different direction than she had planned. She seems a little (or a lot) too controlling. I find myself rooting for her characters to fight back and assert themselves. In fiction, as in life, obedient people are sort of wimpy.

Up to this point, I've discussed *Sula* largely according to my standards; to be fair to Toni Morrison—and to better understand her book—we should look at TM's novel in light of her own standards. How does *Sula* fare against TM's own list of goals?

**1.** A participatory quality between book and reader
> Quite; it's a chatty book, but again (in my opinion), the chat would be more intimate if it were told by one person instead of a whole bunch.

**2.** An aural quality in the writing
> Spectacularly so; the writing (especially Part One) is super-condensed, spoken poetry; TM had not yet eliminated adverbs (softly, loudly, etc.) in *Bluest Eye,* but she does here.

**3.** An open-endedness in the endings of her books that is agitating
> Sort of; great book, very good ending, but they don't exactly match.

**4.** An acceptance of and keen ability to detect subtle differences
> This strikes me as frighteningly close to a recipe for racism. I'm sure that every racist in the world is proud of his "ability to detect subtle differences." Feel free to apply this one if you like, but I'm going to ignore it from now on.

**5.** Acknowledgment of a broader cosmology and system of logic
> Yes, but it's small potatoes, rigged, and unsubtle as a "plague of robins."

**6.** A functional as well as an aesthetic quality

> It's functional in a didactic sense (i.e., it "sells" a moral point of view); the epiphany in #10 below was enormously "functional" for me.

---

**Epiphany:**

a spiritual event in which the answer to a question is revealed in a sudden flash of knowing.

---

**7.** An obligation to bear witness

> No (not yet; that'll come in her later work).

**8.** Service as a conduit for the "ancestor"

> No (same as above).

**9.** Uses of humor that are frequently ironic

> On nearly every page of Part One.

**10.** An achieved clarity or epiphany and a tendency to be prophetic

> The epiphany I experienced during this book convinced me that my approach to TM's novels had to be personal and totally honest. My father died about ten years ago. At his funeral, I howled like a dog. I think I could have stopped, but I didn't; I'm pretty sure that I chose to act like a maniac. Not until I read a line from *Sula* did I finally understand why I had howled like a wounded animal at my father's funeral. In Toni Morrison's clarifying words—"Good taste was out of place in the company of death." An achieved clarity? An epiphany? Oh yeah. Thank you, Toni Morrison, for the insight. (Damn right, it's personal.)

**11.** A novel that would take her people through the pain and denial of their racially haunted history to a healing zone

> Not yet (that, too, will come in her later work).

## AND THE LANGUAGE . . .

Dear God, the language the woman uses. Most people live in a world filled with objects and we invent words to name those objects. Morrison lives in a world where God created Words . . . Some time later, objects were created to fit the words. In Morrison's world, the beginning of the Bible isn't metaphorical, it's literal: "In the beginning was the Word. . . ."

After the first half of *Sula,* my feelings about Toni Morrison's language were plain and simple: the woman is the greatest line-to-line writer in English since Shakespeare. Most great line-to-line writers are great at either the fancy stuff or the simple stuff; Morrison is magnificent at both. There is a line from *Sula* that has the elemental purity of the best of the Bible:

> They spoke, for they were full and needed to say.

A line like that shouldn't be spoken—it's so beautiful you should sing it.

Then you should light a candle or a piece of incense and thank whatever God you believe in that a writer of such words exists.

*If you want to be a whole man,
you have to deal with the whole truth.*
　　　—MACON JR., TO HIS SON MILKMAN, *SONG OF SOLOMON*

*Where thou diest, I will die.*
　　　—RUTH 1:16

# SONG OF SOLOMON
*(1977)*

Toni Morrison's novel *Sula* had attracted a great deal of attention precisely because of its strong female characters. Instead of playing it safe and cranking out another Women's Novel, Toni Morrison decided to write "a novel informed by the male spirit." That wasn't the only new ground it broke: instead of being a Neighborhood Novel like her two previous books, it was a Tonimorrisonized Generational Novel. And instead of ending with monumental sadness like her other books, it ended on a note of hope, redemption, even spiritual transcendence. (At least that's what some people thought.)

It was ironic that Toni Morrison should write what may be her most readable and life-affirming book at a time when her personal life was so brutal. She had money problems. Her oldest son was entering manhood with a bit too much energy. And her father had died. As she worked on her new novel, she carried on long conversations with her father in her head. She needed his help to write this difficult new book about men, their "attraction to violence," and "the driving forces behind them."

And what a book it is. She called it *Song of Solomon.* It is one those rare creatures: a work of art and a great read. It is so full of life that it spills over the edges onto anyone who reads it.

*Song of Solomon* is more complex than TM's earlier books. The story will be clearer if you know the characters. The characters in *Song of Solomon* are some of the most memorable in fiction. And as we've come to expect from Mizz Morrison, each character—men, women, and even streets—has a story . . .

## Character Bios

**Mr. Smith** = insurance agent who tries to fly from "No Mercy" Hospital across Lake Superior.

**Milkman** (Macon Dead III, called Milkman by everyone but his parents). = One of the definitions of a novel is that it's a kind of fictional biography in which the main character undergoes an important change; Milkman is that character. The novel covers Milkman from his birth (in 1931, the day after Mr. Smith's "takeoff") to age 32, when he apparently undergoes a profound spiritual transformation.

**Macon Dead II** (called Macon or Macon Jr.) = Ruth's husband, Milkman's father; a hard man who despises his wife, disdains his daughters, and after a hateful start, treats his son Milkman with astonishing respect; he's a landlord whose only desire in life is to acquire things. Despite being cast in the role of bad guy, he's a fascinating character. The locals think he's exactly like a white man! In the immortal words of Mrs. Baines: "A nigger in business is a terrible thing to see."

**Ruth (Foster) Dead.** = Macon's wife, Milkman's mother; she's a character you don't know whether to pity or despise. She's a Victim (TM saves her greatest contempt for Victims), then in one sentence, Ruth finds her own poetry—"What harm did I do you on my knees?"—and you kind of love her. As a human being, Ruth isn't much; as a character in fiction, she's as good as it gets.

**Dr. Foster** = The (creepy) father of Ruth Dead; the only colored doctor in town until his death of (fairly) natural causes in 1921, fourteen years before the novel opens; Dr. Foster's story is told in a series of mini-stories that tell of the past.

**Not Doctor Street** = The city wouldn't officially name the street where Dr. Foster lived "Doctor Street" so the locals, not to be denied, refer to it as Not Doctor Street. In most novels it would be absurd to call a street name a character, but Morrison invests it with so much character that it would be a sin not to.

**Magdalene (Lena)** = Milkman's sister, 14 years older.

*continued*

## Character Bios

**First Corinthians** = Milkman's sister, 13 years older (is that a beautiful name, or what?).

**Macon Dead I** ("old" Macon Dead; originally Jake). = Macon Jr.'s father, Milkman's grandfather. A proud man with a brutally ironic sense of humor—especially when it came to names: his own, his daughter Pilate's (chosen at random out of the Bible), his farm (Lincoln's Heaven), his horse (President Lincoln). He was killed when Macon Jr. and Pilate were youngsters. Since then he has been his daughter Pilate's mentor.

> *He looked like all them pictures you see of Africans.*
> *A Pennsylvania African. Acted like one too.*
> *Close his face up like a door.*

**Pilate Dead** = Macon Jr's sister, Milkman's aunt (and spiritual mother); she's just like any other woman who wears her name in a snuffbox earring, carries a sack of bones, raps with her dead father, loves life like a boxful of puppies, and don't take no shit.

> *It was the absence of a navel that convinced people*
> *that she had not come into this world*
> *through normal channels.*

**Reba Dead** = Pilate's dim-bulb daughter, lives from orgasm to orgasm, has great luck until she needs it.

**Hagar Dead** = Reba's daughter, Pilate's granddaughter, Milkman's lover.

**Guitar Baines** = Milkman's best friend, a shining star of a young man who undergoes transformations that some readers (this one included) find highly implausible.

**Henry Porter** = Macon Jr.'s tenant (among other things).

**Freddy** = handyman, town gossip, a gold-toothed bantamweight, the originator of Milkman's nickname.

**Circe** = midwife: delivered Macon, watched Pilate birth herself; helps Milkman unravel the family history.

*continued*

---

### Character Bios

**The Seven Days** = A secret group of black men who avenge the deaths of innocent blacks in a unique way.

**Reverend Cooper** = a preacher in Pennsylvania who helps Milkman locate a cave.

---

# *Song of Solomon*

*Song of Solomon* starts out as a kind of "generational-via-rear-view-mirror novel." Its present tense begins in 1931, the day before Milkman is born, and ends with his spiritual liberation (and perhaps his death) at the age of 32. Counting the excursions into the past—over three generations of the Dead family—the novel covers nearly a century.

The novel opens as Smith the insurance man prepares to fly from the roof of Mercy Hospital clean to the other side of Lake Superior. Two days before the event, Mr. Smith had tacked a note on the door of his house:

> At 3:30 P.M. on Wednesday the 18th of February, 1931, I will take off from Mercy and fly away on my own wings. Please forgive me. I loved you all. (signed) Robert Smith, Ins. agent

Mr. Smith was well-liked (although no one asked him not to jump) and drew a decent crowd, including a pregnant woman and a lady who sang him a song.

Born at "No Mercy" Hospital the day after Smith's attempted flight, Milkman was a gifted child until the age of four, when he learned that people can't fly. Bummed out by that depressing revelation, he grows into a self-absorbed young man who floats through life, committed to nothing, excited by nothing, taking the easy way out of every situation. Milkman works for his landlord father (with very little enthusiasm) during the day and parties (with very little enthusiasm) every night.

Macon rents out apartments in the run-down black area (the Blood Bank, to the locals) and in a fancy white neighborhood nearby. He's a real hardass who collects as much property and "things" as he can manage. Bad as he is to his tenants, Macon is infinitely worse to his wife, Ruth. (When you find out why, you won't exactly blame him.) He is intense about everything except his daughters; he's so indifferent to them that they'd probably be better off if he did hate them. Macon, a fascinating, driven character, tells Milkman why he detests his wife. Instead of appreciating his father's confidence, Milkman is irked because he's been burdened with all that heavy crap about his mother. If Ruth were a bit more innocent and a little less creepy, she'd be a perfect victim, but the more you learn about her, the creepier she gets. When she tells Milkman her side of the story, he's no more sympathetic to her than he was to his father.

Milkman, who moves fast only when he's avoiding responsibility, spends more and more time with his friend Guitar Baines—and with his mystical aunt Pilate, his father's estranged sister. Macon and Pilate had parted ways because of an argument 30-some years earlier after their father was murdered in Pennsylvania. Although his father had forbidden him to see Pilate, Milkman and his energetic buddy Guitar first visited her when Milkman was 12 years old.

> As they came closer and saw the brass box dangling from her ear, Milkman knew that what with the earring, the orange, and the angled black cloth, nothing—not the wisdom of his father nor the caution of the world—could keep him from her.
>
> Of course she was anything but pretty, yet he knew he could have watched her all day. . . .

On the day Milkman met his aunt Pilate, he also met half of her granddaughter Hagar: Milkman had no need to see her face; he had already fallen in love with her behind. They became lovers when he was 17 and she was 22, and they remained lovers for years until he grew as bored with her as he was with everything else. Little by little (one step forward, two peeks into the rearview mirror), we learn that "old" Macon got his peculiar name when he told a drunk Union Army sergeant that he was from Macon, Georgia, and his family was dead. Macon was such an ornery cuss that, for spite, he left the name as it was. He named his daughter by opening the Bible and putting his finger on a word that looked like a tree. He couldn't write, so he drew the word and showed it to Circe, the midwife. Circe told him he couldn't name his daughter "Pilate." Macon, who couldn't read, said, "Like a riverboat pilot?"

> "No. Not like no riverboat pilot. Like a Christ-killer Pilate. You can't get much worse than that for a name. And a baby girl at that."
>
> "That's where my finger went down at."

After old Macon was killed by some white men for his property, Macon Jr. and Pilate thought the killers might do them next, so they hid in a nearby cave. When an old man wandered into the cave, jittery young Macon killed him. Shortly after that, Macon and Pilate discovered gold in the cave. He wanted to take it, she said it was wrong, they had an argument and went their separate ways. Macon

---

### The Story Is One Thing, the Way It's Told Is Another

The novel's storytelling form is unusual, but typical Toni Morrison: secondary characters are given nearly as much space as (and more interesting personalities than) the main character; if a new character enters the story (or an old one needs a new paint job), Morrison stops the story cold (even though the hero might be suspended with one foot on a cliff and another in midair) to tell you about this minor character's parents and his one-eyed philosophical wino uncle and the time he got the measles from the preacher's daughter's music teacher's nephew. Morrison is like the FBI: she has a dossier on everyone. (I think I stole that line from John Leonard.)

With any other writer, you'd throw the book in the garbage; with Morrison, it's, *Do any crazy shit you want to do, just so you keep writing like that . . . and that . . . and that!* I repeat: It is not possible to overestimate the writing of Toni Morrison when she's on her game.

---

eventually went back to the cave, but the gold was gone, so he figured that Pilate had taken it. When he and Pilate met later, she admitted she'd gone back to the cave, but only to get the old dead man's bones. Her father, who visited her regularly, told her it was wrong to "just leave a body," so she went back and got the bones (she still carries the bones with her), but she said the gold was gone. Macon didn't believe it. He was certain she had the gold, so although he had been like a father to her for the first 12 years of her life, he did his best to hate her for the next 30 years. Pilate, barely into puberty when she and Macon split up, spent time in a lot of places, but sooner or later someone would discover she didn't have a navel and people would treat her like a freak. She got tired of that crap, and with the help of her father—her mentor despite the fact that he had died—Pilate started from scratch . . .

> [S]he threw away every assumption she had learned and began at zero. First off, she cut her hair. That was one thing she didn't have to think about any more. Then she tackled the problem of trying to decide how she wanted to live and what was valuable to her. When am I happy and when am I sad and what is the difference? What do I need to know to stay alive? What is true in the world? . . . Throughout this . . . one conviction crowned her efforts: since death held no terrors for her (she spoke often to the dead), she knew there was nothing to fear.

Meanwhile, back in the present tense . . .

Guitar confesses to Milkman that he is a member of The Seven Days, a secret organization that avenges the killing of innocent black people in a unique way. Guitar, who seems to have undergone a serious psychological transformation since we last saw him, bitches Milkman out for not being "a serious person." After his parents had been kind enough to share their dirty laundry with him, Milkman had just about all the seriousness he could stand. Milkman (in his early thirties!) can't take the pressure (what pressure?), he tells his dad he wants to get out of town, he wants Macon to support him for a year or two. Macon tells his son about the gold that he still thinks Pilate stole. The gold would solve Milk's problems and give Macon's fortune a wee boost.

Meanwhile, Hagar is not handling Milkman's rejection of her very well. To quote one of the beauty parlor ladies, "Must not be working out if she's trying to kill him." (I'm still trying to figure out whether that lady is witty or brain-damaged.)

Milkman and Guitar team up to get the gold. Pilate doesn't have it, so they decide that it must still be in the cave in Pennsylvania. Guitar wants to help look for the cave, but Milkman wants to do it alone. To locate the cave in Pennsylvania, Milkman has to go first to Virginia where the family was previously from.

At the point when Milkman begins looking for the cave, the book becomes a "quest novel," like a man in search of the Holy Grail. The search becomes a detective story, with Milkman traveling through Pennsylvania and Virginia, asking questions, piecing together clues. Along the way, Milkman encounters the easy friendship of people in one small town, then offends a local guy in another town without knowing what he did wrong (even though it ends up in a fight), goes hunting with some other guys who might be friendly or deadly, he's not sure which, but a man's gotta do what a man's gotta do. He has a nice little two-night stand with a lovable lady named Sweet. The words with which Toni Morrison describes it turn a list of innocuous behaviors into a definition of love:

> She put salve on his face. He washed her hair. She sprinkled talcum on his feet. He straddled her behind and massaged her back. She put witch hazel on his swollen neck. He made up the bed. She gave him gumbo to eat. He washed the dishes. She washed his clothes and hung them out to dry. She kissed his mouth. He touched her face. She said please come back. He said I'll see you tonight.

Guitar turns up, acting like he's had a lobotomy, trying to kill his former best friend. Milkman does not find gold; but what he does find is his family's history, both in fact and feeling. As he travels through the South, one of Milkman's clues to his background comes from the "Song of Solomon," a nursery rhyme he overhears some kids singing as they play a game in a little Virginia town. The song is a lot like the one Milkman had heard Pilate sing when he was a child:

> Sugarman done fly away
> Sugarman done gone
> Sugarman cut across the sky
> Sugarman gone home.

But these kids in Virginia don't say "Sugarman," they use the name "Solomon." Milkman realizes that the song is part of his own family history, that the "Solomon" in the song is his great-grandfather, a slave who, according to legend, escaped his bondage by flying back to Africa. The novel ends with . . . if you don't know, you don't want me to tell you. You want to read it for yourself (. . . and even then you might not know).

. . . and dozens, literally dozens, more.

*Song of Solomon* was a rich, full novel that overflowed with enough people and stories to keep most writers busy for two lifetimes. It had to be a great success. You don't often see a novel that's literary enough for the fancy-minded and so open-armed and welcoming to anyone with enough energy to open it. All you had to do was open it—the book was so readable it damn near read itself for you.

I've told you the highlights of the main story (Milkman's quest), but I've left out the small stories that make the novel such a delight:

- How Milkman got his name
- The layer upon layer of Ruth's story with her father
- . . . and with her husband
- . . . and with her son
- . . . and with Pilate (who was responsible for Milkman's birth)
- A great scene in which Pilate "reasons" with Reba's lover

## How Did the Critics Like It?

A delight, full of lyrical variety and allusiveness . . . peopled with an amazing collection of losers and fighters, innocents and murderers, followers of ghosts and followers of money, all of whom add to the pleasure of this exceptionally diverse novel.

—Neil Millar, *Atlantic*

If her other novels circle, and they do, *Song of Solomon* (1977) soars—from Not Doctor Street and No Mercy Hospital on Detroit's Southside, "where even love found its way with an ice pick; to a ruined plantation, a cave of the dead and a witch named Circe on the Susquehanna; to Shalimar, on nobody's map of Virginia, where everybody's name is Solomon and the children sing a riddle-song that proves on its decoding to be all about how you can ride the very air to Africa."

—John Leonard, *Nation*

The 'Song . . .' [in] the title of Toni Morrison's third novel is a variant of a well-known Gullah folktale about a group of African-born slaves who rose up one day from the field where they were working and flew back to Africa. In the novel, this tale becomes both the end of, and a metaphor for, the protagonist's identity quest. . . . In basing Milkman's identity quest on a folktale, Morrison calls attention to one of the central themes in all her fiction, the relationship between individual identity and community, for folklore is by definition the expression of community—of the common experiences, beliefs, and values that identify a folk as a group.

—Susan L. Blake, *"Folklore and Community in* Song of Solomon*"*

Toni Morrison's first two books . . . were strong novels. Yet, firm as they both were in achievement and promise, they didn't fully forecast her new book, *Song of Solomon.* Here the depths of the younger work are still evident, but now they thrust outward into wider fields, for longer intervals, encompassing more lives.

*Song of Solomon* isn't, however, cast in the basically realistic mode of most family novels. In fact, its negotiations with fantasy, fable, song and allegory . . . make any summary of its plot sound absurd.

—Reynolds Price, *New York Times Book Review*

## What IS the Book About?

One thing that makes Toni Morrison's novels so much fun is that you can spend hours arguing with friends, lovers, enemies, and yourself about what you just read. What is the book about in a general sense? What is the book's theme or point or meaning? What is the book trying to tell us? As usual, we'll look at the conventional views of the book first.

The sum-it-up-in-a-line description of *Song of Solomon* is that it's the story of Milkman Dead's quest for identity. The two-line version, plus or minus a word, usually goes like this: Milkman, an aimless, self-absorbed young man, starts on a journey to find gold and finds something more important along the way: his family history.

Obviously one of the main themes of the book is Milkman's quest for identity.

In Milkman's case, part of his quest for identity is literal: he wants to find his name.

## *NAMING—the Best Way They Can*

> Naming, after all, is one of the great orchestral themes of *Song of Solomon:*
> If not for a Pilate and a Guitar, Macon (Milkman) Dead would not have
> learned to fly.
>
> —John Leonard, *Nation*

We talked about the fact that every black American whose ancestors were
taken from Africa by force (over 90 percent of present-day African-Americans)
has been robbed of his family name. Your name, and your family name, are
badges of your identity. So finding his name was the first step in Milkman's
quest for identity.

But like everything else in *Song of Solomon,* naming branches out in many
directions. Old Macon named his animals, his farm, his daughter, and himself
as if naming were an act of bitter-humored vengeance. "Down South" names
were like street signs turned the wrong way: if you were one of the locals, you
knew things by their right names; if you weren't, too damn bad. One of the best
little scenes on naming was between Milkman and Guitar. Their friendship is
changing, hovering between trust and suspicion, and they sound like they're
talking to each other from different rooms. In one scene, Guitar gets fed up
with Milkman's self-pity and self-absorption and self-every-damned-thing and
tries to jolt him back to reality:

> "What's your trouble? You don't like your name?"
>
> "No." Milkman let his head fall to the back of the booth. "No, I don't
> like my name."
>
> "Let me tell you something, baby. Niggers get their names the way they
> get everything else—the best way they can. The best way they can."

Naming was the first step in Milkman's quest for identity. Flying was the last.

### Flying—The Myth and the Metaphor

If you asked Toni Morrison what *Song of Solomon* was about, she didn't equivocate.

≈≈≈≈≈≈≈≈≈≈≈≈≈≈≈≈≈≈≈≈≈≈≈≈≈≈≈≈≈≈≈≈≈≈≈≈≈≈≈≈≈≈≈≈≈

It's about black people who could fly. That was always part of the folklore of my life; flying was one of our gifts. I don't care how silly it may seem. It was everywhere—people used to talk about it, it's in the spirituals and gospels.

—*to Mel Watkins, 1977*

≈≈≈≈≈≈≈≈≈≈≈≈≈≈≈≈≈≈≈≈≈≈≈≈≈≈≈≈≈≈≈≈≈≈≈≈≈≈≈≈≈≈≈≈≈

TM stressed the point that this was not an Africanization of the Greek myth of Icarus. It has things in common with the Greek myth, but it is a distinct and distinctly African myth. The version of it we're most familiar with comes from a Gullah folktale (Gullah refers to people from the islands off the U.S. East Coast, mainly North Carolina. Blacks who lived there kept their African heritage more intact than at any other place in the Americas.) Milkman's flying is not just literal—it's a metaphor for his identity quest.

The Myth of the Flying Africans in *Song of Solomon* would mark the first (but definitely not the last) time that Toni Morrison designed a novel around myth and folklore.

### Ancestry and Community

Honoring one's ancestors, one of the foundations of African philosophy, is a virtual trademark of Toni Morrison's fiction, but she didn't deal with the issue until *Song of Solomon*. People like Pilate and Circe almost literally live in a community with their ancestors (Pilate constantly talks with her dead father), but Milkman starts out with no connection to anyone or anything. Almost by accident, in the process of searching, Milkman begins feeling a connection to the people around him. For the first time, he feels a connection to the community. Even a bit of responsibility for the community. (I won't lie to you: I read about Milkman's sense of responsibility in TM's interviews or in essays by various critics but I didn't feel it when I read the book.)

I didn't see any real evidence of his love either, but this is the conventional view . . .

### LOVE (or a Two-Night Stand Sung by Caruso)

Milkman learns so much in a very short time. He learns how to love some-body, nicely, tenderly, give something in return. . . .

—Toni Morrison to Mel Watkins

> She put salve on his face. He washed her hair. She sprinkled talcum on his feet.

Maybe, when you write like Toni Morrison, sometimes your words are so beautiful they seduce you into thinking you can turn a two-night stand into love. There's love coming from all over *Song of Solomon*—the book reeks with love—but Milkman's two-nighter? (Hell, if that's love, I've been too hard on myself for all those jitterbuggin' years!)

There was so much love in the novel: Ruth's crazy father-love, Hagar's sad love, Pilate's universal love . . . and the language. There is love coming right out of the words . . . and back into the novel from our love for her words.

### WORDS . . . When the Language Is Right

And sometimes, when the language is right . . . I begin to react to the char-acters who say certain things. In *Song* when Milkman's mother says to his fa-ther, "What harm have I done you on my knees?" then I loved her. I felt all kinds of chilling things. When the language fits and it's graceful and power-ful like I've always remembered black people's language to be, I'm ecstatic.

—Toni Morrison to Mel Watkins

Other of her books have long stretches of wonderful writing but *Song of Solomon* is Toni Morrison's most finely written book from cover to cover. And something about the language seems to celebrate life more than the others. About that quote in her interview with Watkins—

- TM gets the wording slightly wrong: "What harm did I do you on my knees?"
- And she gets the "receiver" wrong: Ruth said it to Milkman, not his father.

(I am not some nitpicker who considers those tiny mismatches "mistakes"; I consider them strongly suggestive evidence (but not irrefutable proof) of what TM does & doesn't consider important in her novels: she falls in love with the words; almost doesn't give a damn who they're spoken to; and, by her example, "tells" us that it is less important to be literal about the words, than it is to understand the spirit of them so thoroughly that you can improvise on them.)

I felt the same way when I read it: I loved Ruth and every once in awhile I try to tell myself that there is no Ruth, no Pilate, no Macon . . . there are only words. Are scientists who create life in test tubes any more miraculous than a writer who creates living human beings with words?

## Symbolism and Guitars

There was loads of everything in this novel, including Symbolism. (Symbolism is peculiar stuff. Either you like it or you don't. I usually don't.) Examples from TM Herself:

*S*YMBOLS / SYMBOLISM  ≈≈≈≈≈≈≈≈≈≈≈≈≈≈≈≈≈≈≈≈≈≈≈≈

- "This man, Milkman, has to walk into the earth—the womb—in that cave, then he walks the surface of the earth and he can relate to its trees—that's all very maternal—then he can go into the water, which is untrustworthy, then he can bathe and jump into the water, then he can get to the air."
- "Pilate is earth. Her brother is property."

—*to Anna Koenen, 1980*

≈≈≈≈≈≈≈≈≈≈≈≈≈≈≈≈≈≈≈≈≈≈≈≈≈≈≈≈≈≈≈≈≈≈≈≈≈≈

To me, when a writer talks like that about her characters, she diminishes them. She may as well hang picket signs on them (but *she's* the one with the Nobel Prize). *Song of Solomon* had as much symbolism as one of those Translate-Your-Dream books that TM's grandmother used to bet the numbers. Pilate's house (with Reba & Hagar) was the Maternal Household where everyone was free and equal; Macon's house was the Paternal Household, arranged in a hierarchy from Boss to Invisible. Pilate is Milkman's Spiritual Mother; Ruth is his Natural Mother. Ruth is Prisoner; Pilate is Free. Macon is a Taker; Pilate is a Nurturer. Flying is Freedom, Emotional/Spiritual Emancipation (no one can give you that, you have to give it to yourself). Guitar is . . . Guitar is . . . damned if I know. (I think he was Symbolic of a Man with a Different Personality on Every Page . . .)

Speaking of Guitar: There were two things people complained about—Guitar and the ending. Susan Lardner, writing in the *New Yorker,* expressed perfectly what many felt:

- "I have to admit having trouble figuring out the full purpose of . . . Guitar."
- "his conversion from Milkman's closest friend . . . into his nemesis [is] a puzzle to me."

. . . I was even more confused about The Seven Days than I was about Guitar. I have a high tolerance for ambiguity, but The Seven Days confused the bejesus out of me. Guitar and Milkman talk, discuss, argue about The Seven Days for a couple hundred pages, but you never know (or at least I never knew) how you were supposed to take it. Are these guys Batbro' and Robin or a bunch of psychos?

(Much to my amazement, I woke up a few mornings ago with an insight that helped me make perfect sense of both Guitar and The Seven Days. I'll 'splain it in a minute.)

## Death and Ambiguity

Pilate seemed to have found the right way to deal with everything, including death. She regularly talked to her father, her mentor, even though he had died years ago; she had no fear of death; she thought there was a good possibility that you didn't have to die if you didn't want to; she mourned the death of her daughter without restraint; and she gave her life without hesitation for Milkman.

Why, you may ask, am I not dealing with Milkman's death? Death? What death?

Toni Morrison told some interviewers that she never believed that Milkman and Guitar would kill each other. She thought they'd be like rams that crash into each other like a pair of Volkswagens.

If I'm not mistaken, Toni Morrison was the only person in the universe who thought that they wouldn't kill each other. I wish they had "like antelopes, locked horns." But there was no evidence of that in the book. A lot of people didn't like the ending.

"Many readers decry . . . the deliberate ambiguity of Morrison's conclusion."

—Jan Furman, *Toni Morrison's Fiction*

## IT'S MY TURN NOW

I have some different thoughts on *Song of Solomon*. Some of them strike me as so true and obvious that I'm surprised that nobody has said them. (Maybe they have and I just don't know about it.) For the most part, I think that Toni Morrison's books are poorly interpreted. I think that one of the main reasons that the interpretations of Morrison's novels tend to be lame (and so uniform they scare you) is that people pay way too much attention to what TM says about her own books. Most writers are lousy judges of their own work (and TM is worse than most), but so what? She wrote the book—do we expect her to judge it for us too? What is *Song of Solomon* about? It's about abundance. It's about overflowing with life, it's about spilling over the edges of whatever is trying to contain you. It's about overflowing with so much of everything, including meanings, that you have no excuse not to make up your own damn mind what it's about. I'll give you a few more options: Ignore them and replace them with ideas of your own. Let's boogie—

### What Song of Solomon *Told Me*

I tried to read *Song of Solomon* the way TM said she'd like us to read her books, to go into the novel and be with the characters, instead of staying on the outside looking in.

I didn't have to go in: the novel sucked me in. I couldn't have stayed outside if I'd wanted to. With Morrison's other novels, I forced myself to take notes as I read. With *Song of Solomon* the notes quickly became a drag. There are lots of books I like, but not many that I love. I wasn't going to let a stinking pencil stand between me and a ride on Morrison's Mighty Cloud of Joy. Somewhere around page 20, I put down my pencil.

The last thing I wrote says it all:

F—ING MORRISON WRITES EVERY LINE LIKE IT'S THE END OF THE WORLD!

I promised myself I'd take notes later and disappeared into the book.

. . . what I came out with was much different than TM or the critics described. It was like I'd read a completely different book. I'm going to tell you what (I think) *Song of Solomon* is about. Not only that: At least one of the things I tell you that the others have ALL wrong, I'd bet my brother's left lorenzo that you'll agree with me. (I'll just be telling you what you already know.)

### Like Henry-the-Something—Part 3

A few hundred years ago, Brother Shakespeare wrote two plays that he thought were about a historical honkie named Henry-the-Something. In the process of writing about ol' Henry-the-Something, Shakespeare had created a secondary character, a mere supporting player, called Falstaff. A supporting character should know his place and stay in the background where he belongs. But this whacky fat knight Falstaff seemed to have a mind of his own. No matter how hard Shakespeare tried to shove Falstaff into the background, Falstaff, because of the beauty and the power and the life-loving force of his one-of-a-kind personality, simply stole the whole damned show.

The way I see it, that's exactly what happened with Pilate.

Toni Morrison can tell me till her nose falls off that Milkman is the Star of *Song of Solomon,* but I'm not buying it. No matter what Toni Morrison intended, WE know that Pilate was the heart, soul, and spiritual center of *Song of Solomon.* Milkman, bless his dull little ass, had the charisma of a loaf of bread. Let me stop and emphasize our point:

Pilate was, by every meaningful definition of the term, the Main Character.

The minute Pilate walks into the novel, the page lights up like God was shining a flashlight behind it. (You felt that, I know you felt it . . . you just didn't trust your feeling. You didn't trust your self. You let all those jive "authorities" talk you out of the authority of your own soul.) Pilate was the standard against which we judged the other characters (and ourselves): an intuitive genius, a passionate humanist, a friend who will visit you even after you die; a mother who will protect you from a bad man without forgetting that the bad man has a mother too. Every time Pilate left the book, she left a hole no one else could fill. I get the feeling that sometimes TM's characters outgrow the original plan she had for the book—but she forces them to conform to it. Despite Morrison's efforts to control her, Pilate was the heart, soul, and spiritual center of the book.

(NOTE: When I said "I know you'll agree with me" or "I'm going to tell you what you already know," it was only in reference to naming Pilate as the real star of the show.)

> **Toni Morrison Talks to Nellie McKay**
>
> **Morrison:** Sometimes a writer imagines characters who threaten, who are able to take the book over. To prevent that, the writer has to exercise some kind of control. Pilate in *Song of Solomon* was that kind of character. She was a very large character and loomed very large in the book. So I wouldn't let her say too much.
>
> **McKay:** In spite of keeping her from saying much, she is still very large.

**Q:** If Pilate is the Center of the book, does that mean Milkman isn't?

**A:** No, it doesn't. The way I see the book now, it has two Centers.

**Q:** Why two Centers?

**A:** Because it's two books: A Eurocentric Novel and TM's first real honest-to-God fully formed African-American Novel.

**Q:** Can you prove that?

**A:** Definitely not. But I can show you why I concluded that and you'll decide for yourself.

## Harold Bloom? THE Harold Bloom?

It wasn't all that long ago that Harold Bloom was the most creative literary critic in America, but for the last several years, Bloom's main claim to fame is as a Defender of the Canon, the so-called Greatest Books in the World that, entirely by coincidence, were all written by dead old white guys. Toni Morrison has fought ferociously against the Canon—and against the Eurocentric novel that the Canon judges all books by—so when I spotted an article by Bloom suggesting that *Song of Solomon* was so good that it would one day be part of the Canon . . . I admit: I was a bit suspicious. After comparing TM to Faulkner half a dozen times (just to piss her off, I'm sure), Bloom raps in "professorspeak"

> Milkman Dead, the protagonist of *Song of Solomon,* is a true Faulknerian quester, driven by a metaphysical need for his true name, and for the transcendental folk-values that have been alienated from him because he has been "called out" of that name, as Keith Byerman observes. Milkman's search begins to find fulfillment only when he comes upon the appropriately named Circe, an aged black woman who incarnates a total rejection of all principles and standards that are not African. She sends him to his ancestral American village, Shalimar, where initially he is resented almost as though he were wholly contaminated by the . . . white culture. Later . . . he undergoes a [radical] metamorphosis. . . . There is nothing else in Morrison's work so magically strong (and indeed strongly magical) as Milkman's transformation. It is wholly persuasive. . . .

Is it just me or does that review sound a bit Trojan Horsey to you? *Song of Solomon* is a sprawling, river-with-tributaries-branching-in-all-directions novel. It branches out into mini-novels of Pilate and Macon, Old Macon's naming frenzy, Pilate's journey of self-discovery, Ruth and her strange father, Hagar trying to ice Milkman, Guitar and The Seven Days—and dozens of other wonderful stories that the selectively blind Bloom pretends not to see. Why do you suppose Bloom has focused ONLY on Milkman's "Faulknerian quest" and reviewed it as if it were the entire novel? I'll tell you why: Br'er Bloom's kissy review of *Song of Sol* is actually a promo for the Eurocentric novel in disguise.

## Beware of Critics Bearing Gifts . . .

Bloom isolated Milkman's Quest because, smart cookie that he is, he recognized that Milkman's Quest was a perfect little Eurocentric novel-within-a-novel. By praising it, and only it, he could put a zinger on Toni Morrison even as he praised her novel. (Like, "You can rant about the Eurocentric novel, honey, but it's the only thing worthy of note in your best book!") When you finish reacting to the trash-talking aspect of Bloom's review, note the fact that Bloom realized that if you separate Milkman's Quest from the rest of the book, it is a perfect Eurocentric novel.

## Why Is That Important?

Because once you realize that Milkman's Quest is a Eurocentric Novel, things that didn't add up suddenly make perfect sense: like Guitar and The Seven Days. All you have to know about the Euro-Novel is the bare essentials (see sidebar). I'll give you details as we go.

> ### Recipe for the Eurocentric Novel
>
> **1.** A Hero (Milkman) who REALLY wants something (Gold, to find the Cave, family History . . .) "McGuffin" is a dopey word Alfred Hitchcock uses to describe whatever the Hero is chasing: gold, a cave, family history, ticking time bomb, microchip. Hitchcock says they're interchangeable: a suspense story needs one. In Extreme cases, the Hero will kill to get the McGuffin—and die if he doesn't get it.
>
> **2.** The Hero goes after the McGuffin, but some Obstacle (local yokels, broken car, missing info) keeps him from getting it. He overcomes that obstacle; then another obstacle gets in his way and another, etc.
>
> **3.** The Last Obstacle (Guitar and gun) is the toughest of all. Either the Hero overcomes that Obstacle and gets his McGuffin or he loses it forever . . . . In extreme cases, he dies.

## How Do We Explain Guitar?

Why did this bright young guy, Milkman's best friend, turn into a robotic madman and try to kill him? Was it for some deep psychological reason? No. Guitar went nuts because of the structure of the Eurocentric novel! It goes like this. If you look at the ingredients of the Euro-novel, you'll see that you need three things: the Hero (Milkman), the McGuffin (cave, family history) and Obstacles. The Last BIG Obstacle should be a Person who's such a Bad Ass that the Hero will be the Underdog. He should also be someone we know (it's cheating to bring in major players late in the game). But Milkman is in a strange town, hundreds of miles from home, badly in need of a Last BIG Obstacle, and none of the locals qualify for the job. So what do you do? You import one from home. Someone we know well. Like Guitar. But he's too sane and principled to shoot his best friend. Then make him IN-sane and UN-principled. Any decent Eurocentric Novel needs an Obstacle and Guitar was going to be IT, even if we had to relocate him and "modify" him. How do we modify him? We invent a group. What kind of group?

### Any Kind of Group, Just So It Has the Following Characteristics:

- It must have enough of a good side and a rational enough justification so that we don't automatically write off anyone who joins it as totally nuts.
- It must be bad enough so that when Guitar does snap, it automatically stands as a sort of we-should-have-seen-it-coming "explanation."
- It must have guns. One of the suggestions for a Well-Made Plot: "If you want to shoot somebody in Act 3, you have to put a gun on the table in Act 1."

So, while *The Seven Days* doesn't compute as a group of toxic avengers, it makes perfect sense as a fictional device invented (1) to give Guitar an excuse for his busted personality; (2) to provide an "objective" reason (orders from the group) for Guitar to ice Milkman (they thought he squealed on Henry Porter); (3) and to "put guns on the table" in Act One.

### Aren't the Kind of Things You Just Explained Mainly for Writers?

No. They're important for anyone who wants to understand a novel. A novel operates on different levels. We usually talk about plot and characters and other "word" things. But a novel also operates on a level someplace between architecture and music. (You construct it like architecture, but you feel [or hear] a kind of CLUNK when it's wrong—like a bad note in music.) Before I figured those things out, Guitar and The Seven Days seemed to screw up the logic of the book. Not my logic, the book's logic—the book's *musical* logic. Something in the book went CLUNK. When I figured it out, I realized that it was going CLUNK because I was expecting human-psychology logic (Guitar) and coherent-actions logic, I listened to it with the . . . right set of ears, and it sounded absolutely beautiful. When I figured out those things for myself: clarity, epiphany, and participation in the novel in one big BANG! Try to figure things out for yourself.

## SONG—TM's FIRST FULLY REALIZED AFRO-AMERICAN NOVEL

I don't think it makes sense to take the position that TM has to actualize all of the characteristics of the African-American novel in one book before you can say she pulled it off. I think *Song of Solomon* stands as TM's (or anyone's) first fully realized African-American novel. According to my tally, she nailed nine out of 11 of her stated goals.

- It was intimate.
- It read better than spoken words, it read like music.
- It brought you into it as a participant.
- TM's language brought me epiphanies and Pilate's wisdom brought clarity.
- It acknowledged a broader cosmology than the narrow scientific world view.
- It not only honored its ancestors, that was one of its main themes: Pilate and Circe almost literally "live" with their ancestors (Pilate constantly talks with her father); Milkman's quest is essentially a search for his ancestors.
- It was a feast of ironic humor: the most obvious examples are the names old Macon gave his farm (Lincoln's Heaven) and his horse (President Lincoln).
- It was functional in the sense that it meant to teach you something: Pilate's list ("she threw away every assumption she had learned and began at zero") and, some say, Flying—but I skipped that one, thank you!

■ And TM's ending certainly agitated a lot of people (though I'm not sure if it was in the way she intended).

*Song of Solomon* actualized every goal but two that TM had dreamed into her Afro-American novel ideal: (1) an obligation to bear witness and (2) a novel that would take her people through the pain and denial of their racially haunted history to a healing zone.

It would take her another ten years to bring home those last two goals. And she would do it with one of the most powerful books by anyone, ever. But let's stay in this novel. I do look at *Song of Solomon* as two novels: an African-American novel (emphasis on the African); and a Eurocentric novel (I don't think you have to look at it that way). I think that Milkman was the center of one novel and Pilate was the center of the other. I much preferred Pilate and her novel to Milkman and his. Among other things, I thought that the "suspense" TM tried to generate for Milkman's quest was forced

> **A Mere Human vs. the Forces of Nature**
>
> In Milkman's defense, he was doomed by the structure of the novel(s). On one side, you have this cast of characters so watchable, it's like you're not reading a novel—you're watching Fellini and Bergman's film version of the novel, filled with larger-than-life, crazier-than-life characters. More like Forces of Nature than mere humans.
>
> On the other side, you have Milkman, the hero (a very small *h*) of a Novel of Conversion. That kind of novel only works if you start out with the most ordinary, average guy in the world: Everyman. (You don't want a brother who's black, you want one who's GRAY!) So here's this poor, average, everyday guy. How can he be anything but invisible in the same room with all those Forces of Nature?

and artificially prolonged (but the novel as a whole is such a beautiful piece of music, I don't want it to be any other way than it is).

Even so, there are questions I should answer (and others I should ask), mainly about my indifference to Milkman and his quest. I didn't want to do the guy a disservice (even if he was only a character in a novel) so I asked around to see if other people found him dull. My wife had read *Song of Solomon* years ago and loved it. She remembered Old Macon, Macon Jr., Ruth, and several others, but she didn't remember Milkman. She sure remembered

Pilate. Every person I asked had intense feelings for Pilate. Most people remembered Milkman, but very few thought he was anything hot.

Not only did Milkman have an underwhelming personality, but TM didn't give him any good lines. One-Legged Eva (*Sula*) was an ornery old buzzard, but TM gave her such quirky words that she stole the novel. If TM had dressed Milkman in her Sunday language, she could have turned him into a Hero. But as the novel stands now, Milkdud was a boring young man who couldn't fly no matter what TM said about him. And if some Benevolent God of Dull Characters had let him hitch a ride to Africa, he was so dull that the Africans would have sent his sorry ass back!

### What He's Being Converted to Isn't Much to Write Home About

Many novels, including *Song of Solomon,* aim to "convert" the hero to the Religion (political system, ideology) of the Author's Choice. A large part of why I couldn't get interested in Milkman was the "religion" that TM wanted to convert him *to:* go to the small town where your grandparents lived, get to know the locals, and you'll undergo an intense spiritual awakening. With all due respect, that's preposterous! It might make sense in a romance-novel way if you had him go to Africa—but to send him Down South to have a few beers, get punched out, stomp around a cave, have a two-night stand with a local lady? It isn't likely to change your life—unless you die of boredom!

And the Quest itself was lame! There was no pressing need for Milkman to find his family's history, nor did he find anything earth-shattering in that history to justify all the hullaballoo. Milkman spent 200 pages chasing one of Hitchcock's McGuffins!

### We Were Just Kidding about the Flying . . . Weren't We?

And the flying that is the "center" of the novel? It's little more than a frame for the story—a minor and unconvincing one at that. The flying stuff, every detail and hint of it, takes up no more than five or ten pages. If there'd been no mention of flying, would it be a significantly different book? Or a less beautiful book? Not to me. Or if at the end of the book, Milkman had busted out in a big, shit-eatin' grin, given Guitar a high-five, and said, "We know we could fly if we want to—*we just don't want to!"*—would that have hurt the book? Not for me. It might have made it even better.

To me, the ending had a lack of conviction. (A healthy lack of conviction.)

It reminded me of a TV interview I saw with Wyclef Jean, the rapper from Haiti:

> The microphone lady: "Some say that your music has a special power because you're from Haiti and you've lived all your life amidst magic."
>
> Wyclef Jean: "We know that magic is real. We know it is. We live with it every day. Just last week we gathered near the waterfall to witness a ceremony in which a man jumps off a cliff."
>
> "Did the man really jump?"
>
> "Of course. I told you, we live with Magic. It's everyday with us."
>
> "Did you go down to the bottom of the cliff to . . ."
>
> "Are you kiddin' me! I ain't going down there. For all I know, the guy is splattered all over the ground!"

(I guess that means you didn't like the ending?)

Not at all. I found the ending unconvincing, but the fact that Toni Morrison willed a happy ending counted for a lot with me. A book is a world in which the writer is God. I'd much rather have a God that at least tries to make life end in a meaningful way than one who butchers her characters and blames it on reality instead of Herself. I liked the ending just fine. But . . . (But what?)

## SOMETIMES I GO INTO THE NOVEL, SOMETIMES IT COMES INTO ME

MILKMAN said, "You don't believe I could fly, do you?" I answered him honestly and said, No, I didn't, but it wasn't because I thought no one could fly; if TM had told me Pilate could fly, I'd have believed it in a minute. Milkman asked me if I knew why he couldn't fly. I said, No. He said, "Because of my stupid name." He asked me to ask TM how, in a novel that was so sensitive to names, she could have given him a stupid name like "Milkman." "How could I fly with a name like that? It nailed me to the ground."

AND THEN MY FATHER (although he had been dead for ten years) said, "Both of you birds could take a lesson from the lady about honoring your ancestors." Milkman split, I hugged my father, told him it was good to see him. He said, "You look like shit, son. Are you using drugs?" I said, No: he said, "Then maybe you ought to start." I laughed, but not too hard. He asked me how I was going to end this chapter. I showed him part of an article by Susan Lardner from an old *New Yorker*—

And . . . in four pages that would have to be reprinted whole for proper quotation, Morrison describes Pilate bursting into a funeral service with a shout, shifting into a whisper, then a question, then two songs, and then speaking "conversationally" to each member of the congregation, her "words tossed like stones," we are told, "into a silent canyon."

> Suddenly, like an elephant who has just found his anger
> and lifts his trunk over the heads of the little men who want
> his teeth or his hide or his flesh or his amazing strength,
> Pilate trumpeted for the sky itself to hear, "And she was loved."

**Dad:** Kind of makes you want to bow your head, doesn't it, son?

**Ron:** Yeah, dad. It sure does.

**Dad:** The epiphany, the spiritual awakening, the transcendence . . . they're all there.

**Ron:** They sure are . . .

**Dad:** Something's on your mind?

**Ron:** The flying. It means so much to Toni Morrison and so little to me—what am I missing?

**Dad:** Her father had just died. Maybe she wanted to give him the greatest gift she could imagine. Maybe it was him who went flying back to Africa?

*I wish I'd a knowed more people.*
*I would of loved 'em all.*
  —Pilate's dying words, *Song of Solomon*


*The earth does not argue,*
*It is not pathetic, has no arrangements,*
*Does not scream, haste, persuade, threaten, promise,*
*Makes no discriminations, has no conceivable failures,*
*Closes nothing, refuses nothing, shuts nothing out.*
  —Walt Whitman, "A Song of the Rolling Earth"


*(That's what you think, pal!)*
  —Ron David


# Tar Baby
## *(1981)*


## Background

Most of us know the story of the Tar Baby, either from the children's stories about Br'er Rabbit and Br'er Bear popularized by the white American writer Joel Chandler Harris in his Uncle Remus stories or from the animated Disney movie, a full-length cartoon in which birds and butterflies and all of nature sang. What many people may not know is that, like so much of American culture, those stories were "borrowed" from black Americans without so much as a Thank You. Variations of the story of the "trickster" Br'er Rabbit were common in black communities all over the Americas. The stories, which had originated in West Africa, were brought to the new world by the men, women, and children who had been taken by force from Africa. Separated from their homes, families, and culture and treated like animals, they adapted the stories to fit their new situation— slavery, powerlessness, and humiliation. Bre'er Rabbit wasn't some cute cracker cousin of Bugs Bunny—the rabbit always represented the slave. Not a lion or an elephant or some other powerful creature; a rabbit. All he had going for him were his wits, but if he played his cards right . . . Interesting, but what does it have to do with Toni Morrison?

≈≈≈≈≈≈≈≈≈≈≈≈≈≈≈≈≈≈≈≈≈≈≈≈≈≈≈≈≈≈≈≈≈≈≈≈≈≈≈≈

I use that old story because, despite its funny, happy ending, it used to frighten me. The story has a tar baby in it which is used by a white man to catch a rabbit. "Tar baby" is also a name, like nigger, that white people call black children, black girls, as I recall. . . . I found that there is a tar lady in African mythology. . . . At one time, a tar pit was a holy place. . . . [Tar] held together things like Moses's little boat and the pyramids. For me, the tar baby came to mean the black woman who could hold things together. The story was a point of departure to history and prophecy.

—*to Thomas LeClair, New Republic*

≈≈≈≈≈≈≈≈≈≈≈≈≈≈≈≈≈≈≈≈≈≈≈≈≈≈≈≈≈≈≈≈≈≈≈≈≈≈≈≈

## THE STORY: THE GENERIC VERSION

The second thing you notice about Morrison's *Tar Baby* is that you can read a description of the book and have no idea whatsoever what the texture of the book is like. (The first thing you noticed if you read through the first few pages is that it seemed to be written by somebody else.) Summaries of the story generally begin by saying that novel is set on a small fictitious island in the Caribbean, Isles des Chevaliers, named after a group of mythical African horsemen. According to the legend Morrison gives us in her book, the Africans were brought to the island as slaves, but they escaped and were said to be roaming the hills on horseback.

Against this mythical backdrop, Morrison tells a modern love story: Jadine, a beautiful, black model is the niece of Sydney and Ondine Childs, long-time servants of a retired white millionaire named Valerian Street. Valerian, who lives in an estate on the island, has paid for Jadine's French education and he treats her with great respect . . . in stark contrast to the way he treats his ex-beauty queen wife, Margaret. Valerian, richer, smarter, and twenty years older than Margaret, mocks her mercilessly for believing that this Christmas their son Michael will finally come "home" to visit. Jadine captures Michael's spirit (or lack thereof) as she wonders if she should get the 30-year-old cause-a-day social "activist" a Christmas present:

> [I]f she did get him one, it would have to be something earthy and noncapitalistic. She smiled. A loaf of bread maybe?

One evening Margaret discovers a most raggedy intruder hiding in her bedroom closet. She is panic-stricken, but Valerian, who is sometimes too cool for words, invites the intruder to dinner and a sleepover. At first, both Margaret and Jadine are afraid the man might rape or murder them, but (BAM!) Jadine and the man (called Son) fall in love.

During Christmas dinner, Son sets off an argument that ends up involving everyone in the house, shaking each of the characters out of the comfortable roles they'd fallen into. The dark flip sides of their relationships are revealed as reeking with exploitation, mutual dependence, and complicity in unmentionably dirty deeds. The evening ends with Valerian shattered into silence, Sydney and Ondine wondering if they still have jobs, and Margaret mumbling to the moon about her innocence.

Son and Jadine run off to New York. Jadine loves it, but Son finds it unbearable and eventually talks Jade into going with him to the tiny town where he grew up: Eloe, Florida. Jadine, who finds Eloe even more miserable than Son found New York, splits.

In the book's climactic scene, Son rapes Jadine, accuses her of being cut off from her "ancient properties," and tells her the story of the tar baby—like the tar baby, she is something "made" by a white man. The novel ends with Son, unsure whether he can (or wants to) break free from the hold of this beautiful woman "whose face was enough to engage your attention all your life . . . a woman who was not only a woman but a sound, all the music he had ever wanted to play, a world and a way of being in it"—or whether he wants to join the band of mythical horsemen that are said to be tromping around the island?

(Sounds like a fairly easy choice to me!)

## What Did the Critics Say?

For the most part, *Tar Baby* got decent reviews . . . although it seemed that everyone who wrote about it had read a different book. Claudia Tate *(Black Women Writers at Work)* described *Tar Baby* as a sort of racially stressed, symbolic, Jackie Collins love story:

> Morrison's latest novel, *Tar Baby* (1981), is about the evolution of an intimate relationship between an unlikely couple. Jade, a jet-set fashion model, falls in love with a young vagrant only to become estranged soon thereafter. He is not discouraged by their breakup but pursues her with the hope of reconciliation. Through the use of elaborate symbol, Morrison suggests that reconciliation between the black man and the black woman can only occur when they mutually understand they are both victims of racial exploitation.

Dorothea Drummond Mbalia *(Toni Morrison's Developing Class Consciousness)* saw it as a political novel, starring a Pan-African Che Guevera:

> . . . in *Tar Baby* Morrison creates a revolutionary protagonist, Son. . . . Having discovered first the importance of knowing one's history and one's relationship to his people, Son commits himself to sharing this knowledge with other Africans. Thus, by struggling to politically educate Therese, Gideon, Sydney, Ondine, and, in particular, Jadine—symbols of the larger Pan-African society—Son becomes a disciple for African people, a modern-day revolutionary.

Judith Wilson, interviewing TM for *Essence,* contended that Morrison's new novel rattled white folks . . .

> Some white critics who were formerly Morrison's loyal fans seemed startled by *Tar Baby*—it's as though someone they trusted suddenly whipped out a gun and yelled "Power to the people!"

But Ms. Wilson's penetrating, if somewhat defensive, interview strongly suggested that the people it troubled most were young, upwardly mobile black women. Even without TM's challenging answers and assertions, Wilson's questions reveal her unease:

> **Essence:** Can women like Jadine, who have options Black women never had before, reconcile freedom with responsibilities—to elders, men, children?

**Essence:** Isn't that asking for Superwoman?

**Essence:** Jadine . . . seems like the "heavy" in the battle between her and Son. Are you saying that women like her, who are privileged, with a college education and a lucrative career, should feel guilty about themselves in comparison with men who are poor like Son?

As Ms. Wilson's quesions indicate, the most passionate discussions provoked by the book were not about *Tar Baby* as a novel, they were an analysis of the conversations—or debates—that took place IN the novel between Jadine and Son.

If those two made love half as much as they talked, they'd've had 27 children before the novel was over. But for now, let's simply note that one of the things that instantly makes *Tar Baby* feel so different from other Toni Morrison novels is the enormous amount of talk—dialogue. I would guess that, proportionally, *Tar Baby* has about three times as much dialogue as Morrison's other books.

Novelist John Irving's review in the *New York Times Book Review* is quite complimentary. But he seems more annoyed than he lets on when he compares TM's "old-fashioned authorial intrusions" to 19th-century English writer Thomas Hardy, famous nowadays mainly as an example of an author who gave in to his story-killing urges and stopped to lecture his readers in the middle of a novel. When it comes to TM's dialogue, Irving doesn't waffle:

> Less tolerable . . . is her excessive use of dialogue: too much of the story is told through dialogue—and not only through the old couple's conversations. Their niece, Jadine, a super-educated . . . Paris model who "made those white girls disappear. Just disappear right off the page," has a love affair with an escaped criminal, a poor, uneducated north Florida black. . . . Jadine and her lover, Son . . . passionately and violently debate the best way for blacks to be independent of the white man's world. Their arguments are lengthy and become tedious, but they vividly expose the novel's racial tensions.

Despite all the advance hype, many readers felt that *Tar Baby* didn't measure up to TM's normal standards. It felt like something was missing. Even John Leonard, who may be TM's most passionate advocate (and who may also be the best-writing critic in the country) couldn't fall in love with *Tar Baby:* "I fell off the truck with *Tar Baby* (1981). It still seems overly didactic, somehow brittle, her only novel you can't sing. . . ."

*Tar Baby* was the first book by Toni Morrison that I'd ever read—or tried to read.

I couldn't get past the first twenty pages. I've done some thinking since then. But first let's hear from Aunt Remus herself:

## TONI MORRISON TALKS ABOUT *TAR BABY*

### TM tells Thomas LeClair:

> It's a love story, really; the tar baby is a black woman; the rabbit is a black man. . . . He is determined to live in that briar patch. . . . Do you think she would go into that briar patch with him? Well, that's what it's all about.

### TM tells Nellie McKay:

> Many of the problems modern couples have are caused not so much by conflicting gender roles as by the other 'differences' the culture offers. That is what the conflicts in *Tar Baby* are all about. Jadine and Son had no problems as far as men and women were concerned. They knew exactly what to do. But they had a problem about what work to do, when and where to do it, and where to live. These things hinged on what they felt about who they were, and what their responsibilities were in being black.

Later in the interview—

### Nellie McKay asks TM:

> Can you tell me why you ended *Tar Baby* with "lickety-split"?

*Ron David tells Nellie McKay:*

> For God's sake, Nellie, lighten up! It's a cartoon! How else would you end it?

## My Turn, Baby

After *The Bluest Eye* showed us the devastating results of judging people by the way they looked and *Song of Solomon* taught us the importance of naming, what are we supposed to do with a book in which people UN-ironically fall in love based entirely on looks and the hero and his father have generic names (Son and Old Man)? Toni Morrison is one of the best writers in the world. She's too good to write a book as silly and shallow as *Tar Baby* seemed on the surface. What if those of us who didn't love her novel (to say the least) were wrong? What if Toni Morrison has been sitting there with a straight face for 15 years waiting for us brickhead, overliterary bozos to get it? What if *Tar Baby* was a perfectly realized book and everything in it was perfect? Don't read the hype, read the novel. I repeat—

> Forget about what I say in an interview
> —it might be anything—
> but trust the tale and start with that.

(Thank you, m'dear. That's exactly what I'm going to do.)

## Tar Baby
## (The Real Story)

Let's start with the epigraph: The epigraph in front of a novel is like a fortune cookie that sums up the novel's meaning in a few words. So it's worth pursuing.

> For it hath been declared
> unto me of you, my brethren, by them

> which are of the house of
> Chloe, that there are
> contentions among you.
>
> —First Corinthians 1:11

That's real nice . . . but what does it *mean?* First Corinthians is Biblespeak for the first letter that St. Paul wrote to Christians in the Greek city of Corinth, famous for its sexual hanky-panky. Paul was named Saul until a lightning bolt knocked him upside the head and changed his name. Paul is also the patron saint of body-hate. (If thy dingus sins, cut it off.) Jesus didn't chop us into two warring halves (body vs. mind/spirit/soul), Paul did. We've spent two thousand years trying to undo Paul's schizo division and become whole . . . so if I got a letter from St. Paul, I'd seriously consider burning the thing.

But wait a minute: First Corinthians is not only a letter from Paul—it's also the name of one of the characters from Toni Morrison's earlier novel. And Chloe is Toni Morrison's given name. Why would Toni M use a quote "coauthored" by one of her own characters, with her own name in it? Were her intentions serious or humorous?

If they were serious, I'd say that she was on the Mother of all Ego Trips. (Even if she felt like that, she's too savvy to announce it publicly!) I think she was being funny. Being funny and announcing her own ambivalence. The "contentions" that were "among" us were, in fact, within Chloe. Key concepts: Humor and Ambivalence . . .

*Tar Baby* begins and ends with what TM calls "parentheses"—brief descriptions of Son going to the island on a boat. The book inside the parentheses begins with nature "narrating"—telling the story. Parrots and trees and clouds talk, socialize, and have opinions. Everything in nature thinks, speaks, sings, and watches us destroy it. My first impression of that Nature Chorus was that it sounded charmingly silly and Disneyfied, but since I knew that wasn't TM's groove, I presumed it meant to be mystical, serious—instead of Mahler, it was Morrison's *Songs of the Earth.* I thought she'd missed the tone, and the writing was decent for anyone but her, but it was so bold and fearless that I wanted to stand up and applaud. (Damn, she has guts!)

But wait: My working assumption here is that *Tar Baby* was a perfectly realized book. If it seemed to be cartooney, then it was meant to be cartooney. So, with my new aesthetic, *Tar Baby* started out as a cartoon chorus in which nature told us what shitheads we were for messing her up. A Greek chorus by Walt Disney by Toni Morrison provides a running commentary on the action. (BAM!)

That only lasted for a page or two (but it recurred throughout the book).

Unfortunately, it was followed by 59 and a half pages of pure misery. Writing so stinky and bitchy, so miserable and misanthropic, that I had to force myself through it like it was written by Noel Coward with PMS.

Valerian, this inert, above-it-all Candy Millionaire sees a beauty queen on a float in a parade and marries her because she's so very pretty. Eye Candy. She's twenty years younger and so socially klutzy that you feel sorry for her—until the little bimbo refers to Sydney and Ondine as Kingfish and Beulah. This (especially in a book by Toni Morrison) is a woman the reader is clearly not intended to love.

Then, on page 67, Margaret Eye Candy finds the uglified, pre-shower Son hiding in her closet. And from that moment on, the book, while not up to TM's usual standards (we expect her to score a touchdown on every play) was okay. Easy to read . . . even if it did seem superficial and shallow.

But wait: If we're acting on the assumption that *Tar Baby* is a perfectly realized book then, hard as it is to believe, if the first 59 and a half pages of the book were skunky, TM intended them to be skunky! But why would a writer do that? (What can I tell you, Elvis? If clouds can talk and rivers can cry, we're dealing with a whole new block of commandments.) Consider this possibility: If you wanted to write a book that illustrated, demonstrated, proved with the only means at your disposal (words) that the world without black men in it would be an ugly place, devoid of beauty and music and pleasure and tolerance, the most brilliant and convincing strategy you could take—IF you had the guts—would be to begin the book without a black man, and to prove to us how necessary he is to beauty, the beginning of the book, say the first 59 and a half pages before he enters the picture, would be the stinkiest words you could possibly write!

Stinky and shallow and nothing but talk.

(It's an interesting possibility. And if anyone has the guts to do it, it's TM!)

My annoying memory reminds me that Sydney is in the book. Sydney isn't the in-your-face kind of black man we expect nowadays, but that didn't justify excommunicating him from the race. But wait another minute: Margaret had called Sydney and Ondine Kingfish and Beulah. But Margaret wasn't real: she was Eye Candy on a float in a parade with the other fantasy characters. She wasn't bright enough to be bitchy, so if she called them Kingfish and Beulah, maybe she was stating an "authorial" fact. Maybe TM wanted us to think of them as Kingfish and Beulah. This isn't *King Lear* we're dealing with, it's *Tar Baby*, a children's story, a cartoon, a Disney movie where clouds think, rivers talk (and showers transform frogs into princes). The whole damned book is a cartoon.

The whole wonderful book is a cartoon.

The Bad Black Outlaw suddenly appears in Eye Candy's closet! BAM!

She's scared chitless and goes running to her husband, Valerian, named for a pink-and-white flower whose roots herbalists use to put you to sleep. So Kingfish zooms upstairs with a gun to ice the Bad Black Outlaw (who Morrison refers to in the book, I swear, as "literally, literally, the nigger in the woodpile"—an offensive cartoon image, but a cartoon nonetheless; Toni Morrison is playing with us; how could we have missed it?)

Noteworthy Detail: This Gentleman in the Woodpile who'd been hiding in the woods, starving for a couple months—does he steal meat and potatoes or something that a real human being would eat? No way. This starving desperado, I swear to God, steals designer water and chocolate bars! (I'm telling you, it's a cartoon.)

ITEM: Valerian has a greenhouse on a tropical island! Didn't Elmer Fudd or one of those nitwits who chased Bugs Bunny have a greenhouse on a tropical island?

ITEM: Remember when Ondine—Beulah—said that Jadine was so beautiful that her face in a magazine made those white girls fly right off the page? That wasn't a metaphor like we thought it was—BAM!—those white chicks literally flew off the page! Surely you can see that in your mind's eye—you can't help seeing it—woosh!

But it was The Shower that took the cake.

The night that all the nice people discovered the Gentleman in the Woodpile, Margaret was so terrified she didn't sleep a wink; Jade was scared but not enough to miss her beauty sleep; Sydney sat awake all night with a pistol in his lap (I'm not even going to think of Mae West's wisecrack). The following day, as Jadine and Margaret hid out in their rooms, putting their hairdos together to figure out how to get rid of him—unbeknownst to them—the terrifying, dirt-crusted, dreadlocked Gentleman in the Woodpile that they thought was a rapist-slash-murderer biding his time, took a shower.

A shower . . . !

> [A]nd the next time they saw the stranger
> he was so beautiful they forgot all about their plans.

That, my darlin's, must rank as the most magnificent, metamorphistically cosmic shower in the history of fiction. (I checked the cover to see if Fabio was on it!) Here's this guy, uglier than a policeman's armpit, he takes a shower—a shower!—and BAM! honey, he's so gorgeous that brutal island jungles grow soft in his presence, blind chicks drive boats through treacherous waters, and bisexual women go straight!

He and Jadine take one look at each other and, BAM! dreads over heels in love!

And sex like you never had in your (BAM! BAM!) life! (He makes you see stars!)

Why do I believe, from the bottom of my heart, that Son was a cartoon character?

He might have survived the chocolate bars and the designer water. Maybe we could have forgotten the Mother of All Showers after fifty or a thousand pages. But this Gentleman, considered by some a romantic hero and by others a revolutionary and whose half of the dialogue thousands of people take life-and-death seriously, is presented as a man in harmony with nature, in contrast to Jadine's manufactured-by-the-white-man taint, he is the unsullied, natural black man, undamaged by "WEStERn" concepts of work and all that other nine-to-five crap. Son, in other words, is presented to us as some version of . . . call him Ideal African Man with a Few Flaws.

So where does Ideal African Man with a Few Flaws want to take Jadine to wise her up and connect her to her Ancient Properties? To some secret ancestral Yoruba village? To a mountain top in Kenya or a cave in the Serengeti? Maybe even a sacred waterfall in Haiti or some secret little spiritual place in Cuba . . . an after-hours rib-joint in Harlem where Diz and Bird had coffee? Hell, no!

Ideal African Man with a Few Flaws wants to take his baby to Florida . . . Eloe, Florida.

If Son had any credibility at all, Eloe, Florida killed it.

He may as well have taken Jadine to Toledo, Ohio.

After all, one spiritual capital of the world is as good as another.

We can't leave *Tar Baby* without a taste of Toni Morrison's traffic-stoppin' words:

- [H]er sex life had become such a wreck it was downright interesting.

- She didn't want to have any more discussions in which the silences meant more than the words. . . .

- "[I]f ever there was a black woman's town, New York was it. . . ."

- They refused loans at Household Finance, withheld unemployment checks and drivers' licenses, issued parking tickets and summonses. . . . They jacked up meetings in board rooms, turned out luncheons, energized parties, redefined fashion, tipped scales, removed lids, cracked covers, and turned an entire telephone company into such a diamond head of hostility the company paid you for not talking to its operators. The manifesto was simple: "Talk shit. Take none." . . .

- "Oh, horseshit!" she said aloud. It couldn't be worth all this rumination, she thought, and stood up. The avocado tree standing by the side of the road heard her and, having really seen a horse's shit, thought she had probably misused the word. . . .

**[The last 47 words.]**

- The mist lifted and the trees stepped back a bit as if to make the way easier for a certain kind of man. Then he ran. Lickety-split. Lickety-split. Looking neither to the left nor to the right. Lickety-split. Lickety-split. Lickety-lickety-lickety-split.

*Pain penetrates*
*Me drop*
*by drop*
    —SAPPHO

*Denver picked at her fingernails. "If it's still there, waiting, that must mean that*
*nothing ever dies."*
*Sethe looked right in Denver's face. "Nothing ever does," she said.*
    —FROM BELOVED

# BELOVED
# *(1987)*

## WARNING: IF YOU HAVE NOT YET READ *BELOVED*

In many of TM's novels, she "announces" critical information in the first few pages. In *Beloved,* she doesn't. Toni Morrison designed *Beloved* as if the reader had no advance knowledge of either the novel's central tragedy or of the identity of the title character. So if you haven't read *Beloved* and you want to experience it exactly as TM wrote it, don't read past this page.

### On the Other Hand . . .

The reason I decided to write this book was that I knew several people who had started to read one or the other of Toni Morrison's novels, only to put the book down because they had no idea what was going on or they felt intimidated by the book's "literary" style. The novel that was abandoned most often by far was *Beloved.* As good as her first four novels were, *Beloved* is a whole 'nother world, reaching levels of almost impossible beauty. I couldn't bear the idea that there were people who hadn't read *Beloved* simply because they were confused or intimidated by the book's technique. Part of the unique spell the book casts is a powerful need to share it. Above all, I appeal to those of you who tried reading *Beloved* and stopped. If you know two simple facts before you read the novel, *Beloved* is not at all confusing or difficult. (See the "TWO FACTS" sidebar below.) Here's what you need to read a book that will not only "give you dreams"—if you give it half a chance, it just might change your life.

## BACKGROUND

In the early 1970s, while helping Spike Harris gather material for *The Black Book,* Toni Morrison came across an article that she couldn't get off her mind: "A Visit to the Slave Mother Who Killed Her Child." In 1851, a slave named Margaret Garner escaped from a plantation in Kentucky and fled with her four children to a town outside Cincinnati, Ohio. When she was tracked down by her master's slave catchers, Margaret Garner tried to kill her children so that they couldn't be forced into a life of slavery. Only one of the children died, but Garner said she'd rather her children were dead than made slaves and "murdered by piecemeal." What struck Morrison was that even after she was imprisoned for the murder of her own child, Margaret Garner believed that she had done the right thing. She refused to allow her children to suffer as she had done.

One of the characteristics of Toni Morrison's genius is that she sees things in a unique and personal way. Her take on Margaret Garner's suffering is a perfect example: it's so true to the bone that you recognize it's truth the instant you hear it. In Morrison's words, this was "a despair quite new to me but so deep it had no passion at all and elicited no tears" (Century).

For years, Toni Morrison wanted to write Margaret Garner's story but it refused to happen. TM had almost decided that the story couldn't be written; but ultimately, she found her power by surrendering to theirs: "In the end, I had to rely on the resilience and power of the characters—if they could live it all of their lives, I could write it."

Morrison dedicated the book *Beloved* to the "Sixty million and more." Her research (which included a trip to Brazil to look at choke-collars, mouth bits, and other instruments of torture that, for some reason, we don't see in American museums) turned up some astonishing numbers: She asked some scholars to estimate the number of black people who died in 200 years of slavery. "Those 60 million," Morrison said, "are people who didn't make it from there to here."

How do you tell the story of a woman who kills her own child? How can you say anything that isn't shrunk into insignificance by the terrifying logic of the act itself?

A few years before she wrote *Beloved,* TM had written a play, *Dreaming Emmett.* Emmett Till had been shot in the head and thrown into a river for whistling at a white woman. In Morrison's play, Emmett Till came back from the dead to speak on his own behalf . . .

## BELOVED: THE STORY

The year is 1873. The house, known by the locals who carefully avoid it as "124," is located on 124 Bluestone Road on the outskirts of Cincinnati. Sethe (the Margaret Garner character), a former slave on a Kentucky plantation called Sweet Home, has been free for 18 years. Eight years earlier, Sethe's two sons had run away from home. Two months after that, her mother-in-law, Baby Suggs, died. By the time the novel opens, only Sethe and her 18-year-old daughter, Denver, live at 124. Sethe, Denver, and the ghost of a dead baby girl:

> "For a baby she throws a powerful spell," said Denver.
> "No more powerful than the way I loved her," [Sethe replies.]

Sethe flashes back 18 years to the time she traded a stone carver ten minutes of sex to carve the word "Beloved" on her baby's headstone. We aren't told how the baby died. We learn the details in flashbacks. Events in real time are interrupted by memory, but it's reluctant memory. Other flashback novels remember the past; *Beloved* is an attempt to forget it; we get what leaks through the cracks.

In 1873 when the novel opens, the Civil War has been over for eight years and everyone in the book is trying to forget slavery and everything about it. Even Sethe, who faces everything, tries to close off her mind, but her "devious" brain lets chunks of memory through: "Boys hanging from the most beautiful sycamores in the world." Sweet Home, that hateful place, looked so beautiful it made her wonder if hell was pretty too. . . .

On the tail end of that memory, Paul D, also a former slave from Sweet

Home, turns up. When Paul tries to enter the house, he's stopped in his tracks by "a pool of red and undulating light." He remarks on the feeling of evil; Sethe says, "It's not evil, just sad." She asks him to stick around—they (and we) have 18 years of catching up to do. Paul D manages to chase the ghost away. A few days later, a beautiful woman, the age Sethe's baby would have been if she'd lived, comes to the house. She calls herself Beloved. The novel that bears her name and tells her story shuttles back and forth in time, filling us in on the past, moving through the present, and connecting one to the other.

With apologies to Morrison's novel for separating the story from the way it's told, I offer the following sumary since the clearest way to tell the story from this pivot point between past and future—the arrival of Paul D and Beloved— is to go back 30 years and do the "catching up" all at once.

*T*HE *"TWO FACTS" SIDEBAR*  ≈≈≈≈≈≈≈≈≈≈≈≈≈≈≈≈≈≈≈≈≈≈

If you know two facts in advance—one, *Beloved* (the novel) is based on the story of Margaret Garner, the mother who killed her child; two, Beloved (the character) is the dead child returned to Sethe (as if they have some unfinished business between them)—then the novel, complex as it sounds, is not at all confusing. Toni Morrison has rendered the changes in time and place with such story logic that the story unfolds as clearly as if it were told chronologically.

≈≈≈≈≈≈≈≈≈≈≈≈≈≈≈≈≈≈≈≈≈≈≈≈≈≈≈≈≈≈≈≈≈≈≈≈≈≈≈≈≈

Thirty-some years earlier (c. 1840) a pair of "nice" slave owners (with all of the brutal irony that implies) had a plantation in Kentucky called Sweet Home. Paul D, his two brothers (Paul A and Paul F), and Sixo were slaves at Sweet Home when Baby Suggs, a limping old woman, arrived with her lastborn child, her son Halle. The Garners treat the slaves with considerable respect (they call the men "men," value their opinions, let them carry guns) but once they set foot outside Sweet Home, they're "boys" to everyone else.

Garner is nice (but not that nice: he acknowledges their manhood but doesn't free them). He allows Halle to buy his mother's freedom. Baby Suggs wonders why he bothers—what can a crippled old woman do with freedom?— but when she walks through Cincinnati a free woman, she can't believe that "Halle, who had never drawn one free breath, knew that there was nothing like it in the world."

Sethe, 13 years old, arrives at Sweet Home to replace Baby Suggs. The three Pauls and Halle all have their eyes on her (Sixo, the rebel, has his own woman). Sethe marries Halle; they have two sons, Howard and Buglar. A couple years later (around the beginning of the Underground Railroad that helped slaves go north), Mr. Garner dies. Mrs. Garner sells Paul F and lives for two years on the proceeds. Then she frets that she can't run Sweet Home "alone" (i.e., with Sethe, Halle, Paul D, Paul A, and Sixo!), so she sends for her brother Schoolteacher and his two nephews to help her. Unlike Mr. Garner, who treated "his" slaves like semi–human beings, Schoolteacher beats them, measures their body parts to gather "scientific evidence" to support his eugenic racist garbage, and makes "scholarly" lists of their human and animal characteristics (apparently without noticing that his Neanderthal nephews blow the top off of the list of animal characteristics).

The novel asks some hard questions about slavery, like: How do you go about living "freely" after an experience that negates the very concept of self?

The complete erasure of identity has never been so fully dis-expressed as in the list of zeros that add up to Baby Suggs's life. Garner, the "nice" slavemaster, asks Baby Suggs her name:

> "What do you call yourself?"
> "Nothing," she said. "I don't call myself nothing."

In a muted lament that she didn't know if her children were dead or alive or what they looked like or where they were buried, Baby Suggs realizes that, as little as she knew about them, she knew even less about herself—she had no idea what she was like:

> Could she sing? . . . Was she pretty? Was she a good friend? Could she have been a loving mother? A faithful wife? Have I got a sister and does she favor me? If my mother knew me would she like me?

During the first year of Schoolteacher's reign, Sethe's daughter Beloved is born. Sethe and the men can't bear Schoolteacher's cruelty and talk about escape. Sethe, with three children and pregnant with her fourth, can't bear the thought that her children might be sold, so she runs away. She gets her children safely away to Baby Suggs, but she is caught and returned to Sweet Home by the nephews. Sethe is held down by one nephew while the other sucks the milk from her breast. To Sethe, stealing her babies' milk was worse than rape. She tells Mrs. Garner; the nephews find out and beat her bloody.

Sethe sees Paul D strapped into a three-spoke neck collar and looks away to spare him shame. (Eighteen years later, when he turned up at her house, Sethe would learn from Paul D that her husband Halle had been hiding in the loft while Sethe was being molested. The last time Paul D saw Halle, he had gone mad from what was done to his wife while he hid, unable—or in his own harsh self-judgment, unwilling—to intervene.)

Sethe and Halle had planned to escape separately and meet later, but Halle never shows up so Sethe fears he is dead. Pregnant and exhausted, but driven by the idea that her baby needs her milk, she runs away, then collapses. She is saved by Amy Denver, a young white indentured servant on the run to Boston, determined to get some red velvet. Amy nurses Sethe halfway back to health, helps deliver her baby (named Denver in honor of the weird young woman), and zooms off after her velvet.

Sethe makes it to Baby Suggs's house outside Cincinnati. Her sons are healthy and happy, and her baby Beloved is already climbing stairs. Baby Suggs, made ecstatic and holy by freedom, has become a spiritual leader whose passionate love of life, self, and the whole blessed world, transforms those around her. (Baby Suggs is one of the glories of the novel—someone we could all go to school on—until the world caves in on her.)

---

### Quick List of Characters

**Sethe** = Beloved's and Denver's mother; Baby Suggs's daughter-in-law; 14 years old when she marries Halle; 20 when she escapes from Sweet Home; 38 when the novel opens in 1873.

**Beloved** = Bethe's daughter, killed at age two, returns as a 20-year-old woman to confront, love, and ravage her mother.

**Denver** = Sethe's 18-year-old recluse of a daughter.

**Baby Suggs** = Sethe's mother-in-law; Halle's mother; the spiritual leader of the Cincinnati community.

**Halle** = Sethe's husband; Baby Suggs's son; bought Baby Suggs's freedom; so gentle and giving he is doomed under slavery.

*continued*

# Quick List of Characters

**Paul D** = one of the male slaves from Sweet Home; becomes Sethe's lover.

**Sweet Home** = Kentucky plantation where Sethe and the others "worked" as slaves.

**Mr. Garner** = owner of Sweet Home; "nice" slave master.

**Mrs. Garner** = after he dies, she becomes an invalid and sends for her brother-in-law "Schoolteacher" to run Sweet Home.

**Schoolteacher** = brutal slavemaster; a prototypical "scientific" racist.

**Schoolteacher's Nephews** = two sadistic young morons who molest Sethe.

**Sixo** = the bravest and baddest of the male slaves, almost cartoonishly heroic.

**Paul A and Paul F** = Paul D's brothers; Paul F is sold and Paul A is hanged.

**Thirty-Mile-Woman** = Sixo's lover; the mother of "Seveno."

**Amy Denver** = flaky young white indentured servant who helps Sethe deliver Denver.

**Stamp Paid** = an older former slave who runs the ferry boat and survives a brutal life without becoming brutal.

**Ella** = member of the Underground Railroad; she goes from moral to moralistic and back again.

**Underground Railroad** = a string of safe-houses run by brave people to help runaway slaves and free blacks get to Canada.

**The Bodwins** = brother and sister white abolitionists—Quakers, not crackers!

**Janey Wagon** = free black woman; works for the Bodwins and specializes in gossip.

**Lady Jones** = Denver's schoolteacher.

*continued*

---

## Quick List of Characters

**Howard and Buglar** = Sethe's sons; they run away from home in their teens.

**Ma'am** = Sethe's unnamed mother.

---

Sethe, ecstatic about being back with her children, can't believe how much you can love people when you're free. After 28 days of freedom, Sethe sees Schoolteacher riding on horseback into Baby Suggs's yard. Sethe collects "every bit of life she had made, all the parts of her that were precious and fine and beautiful"—her children—and takes them into the shed to kill them so they can't be taken into slavery. She manages to kill only one, Beloved, before Baby Suggs and the others stop her. Sethe is taken away to jail, nursing her baby Denver, as drops of Beloved's blood drip into her milk.

After a few months, Sethe is released from prison. She is avoided by her neighbors, but Sethe doesn't give a damn what they think; the only person who has the right to question her is the baby whose throat she had cut out of pure love.

Sethe gets a job and moves in with Baby Suggs, who by that time, has given up on God. She is ashamed of Him (and of herself) for the events leading to the baby's killing so she spends the rest of her life "pondering colors." Denver starts school, quits when a classmate asks about her mother, and is the first to hear a baby crawling on the stairs—but there is no baby. Mirrors break, furniture flies, baby fingerprints dent the butter. Sethe wonders if they should move to another house, but Baby Suggs says that every house in the country is haunted by "some dead Negro's grief." She says they should be grateful that it is just a baby and not a grown man's ghost.

Howard, Sethe's eldest son, leaves home when the ghost begins shattering mirrors. Buglar holds on until tiny handprints appear in the frosting of a cake. Baby Suggs, worn out and oblivious to everything but color, barely notices the boys are gone; she dies like a run-down battery a few months after they leave. After Baby dies, Sethe and Denver try to entice the ghost to come out in the open, but it won't . . . or can't:

"She wasn't even two years old when she died," Sethe said. "Too little to understand."

"Maybe she don't want to understand," said Denver.

"Maybe. But if only she'd come, I could make it clear to her."

The ghost tips tables, scoots sideboards, and does other spiteful things, but before long Sethe begins to feel that any sign of her beloved child is better than nothing. And once she gets over her fright, Denver realizes that the little hell-raiser is the only friend she has.

. . . Which brings us back to the day the novel opens: Paul D thinks he is doing Sethe and Denver a favor by driving the ghost away, but Denver gets ornery when she realizes that he's chased away her only friend. Denver tries to make Paul feel unwelcome, but he's determined to win her over. There's a carnival in town with white performers; Paul, "breathless with the excitement of seeing white people loose," takes Sethe and Denver to the carnival and spends his last two dollars buying them treats. Then, on the walk home, they discover a beautiful young woman sitting on a tree stump. She can't explain where she's come from. She has a scar on her neck, calls herself Beloved, and she's the same age Sethe's baby would have been if she'd lived. Denver recognizes her almost immediately, but Sethe doesn't seem to have a clue. (Is Sethe really that clueless, or is she repressing it? And is there any difference?)

Paul and Sethe grow closer, as do Denver and Beloved. Paul, protective and suspicious, doesn't trust Beloved and wonders why Sethe lets her hang around. He questions Beloved about her past, but she says she has no idea who she is or where she came from. Denver, who could answer both questions, doesn't.

As Paul D and Sethe negotiate their way from a kind of sexy friendship toward love (although I'm not sure if there's any difference), tiny things become charged with great significance. In an atmosphere where everyone's most passionate need is "beating back the past," when Sethe says to Paul, "You want to tell me about it?" her simple offer to let him "put his story next to hers" is so loaded with love and courage and respect than it almost hurts to read it. (The people in this novel—I don't want to shrink them by calling them "characters"—the people are so monumental and sad and beautiful, that I half won-

### Chronology (Dates Are Approximate)

**c.1518–1850**—the Middle Passage: millions of African men, women, and children die in the Death Ships that take them across the Atlantic.

**1795**—Baby Suggs is born.

**1838**—the Garners buy Baby Suggs and Halle and bring them to Sweet Home.

**1848**—Sethe arrives at Sweet Home; Halle buys Baby Suggs's freedom.

**1849–51**—Sethe marries Halle; they have two sons. • Baby Suggs lives free in Cincinnati.

**1853**—The Underground Railroad begins • Mr. Garner dies; Mrs. Garner sells Paul F.

**1854**—Beloved, Sethe and Halle's daughter, is born.

**1855**—Mrs. Garner sends for Schoolteacher • The slaves plan to escape • pregnant Sethe sends her sons and Beloved to Baby Suggs • Schoolteacher's nephews suck Sethe's breast milk • Paul D, Halle, and Sixo try to escape • Sethe runs away; Amy Denver helps her; Sethe makes it to Baby Suggs's Cincinnati house • Schoolteacher tries to take her back to slavery; Sethe tries to kill her children and goes to jail • Sethe is released from jail, moves in with Baby Suggs.

**1862–63**—Denver (age seven) goes to school; a boy asks about Sethe's jail term; Denver quits school.

**1864**—The ghost first appears; Denver hears it crawling on the stairs.

**1865**—Howard and Buglar leave home • Baby Suggs dies • THE CIVIL WAR ENDS.

**1873**—August: This is where the novel opens • Paul D turns up at 124—Sethe's house • Paul, Sethe, and Denver go to the carnival; on the way home, they discover Beloved sitting on a stump • Autumn: Paul moves out of Sethe's bed • Winter: Beloved seduces him; Paul tells Sethe that he slept with Beloved.

**1874**—Stamp Paid shows Paul a clipping about Sethe killing her child • Paul and Sethe split up.

**1875**—January: Sethe, Denver, and Beloved go ice skating • March: Sethe realizes that Beloved is her dead baby • April: Denver goes looking for work • Summer: the townspeople come to 124 to help Sethe get rid of Beloved.

der if I should turn away rather than invade their privacy.) Paul D tells Sethe about being forced to wear a bit in his mouth like a horse and seeing a rooster that he swore was laughing at him because the rooster was freer than Paul.

For no exact reason, Paul moves out of Sethe's bed. They still make love, but he finds himself sleeping further and further away until he ends up in a cold storeroom. Through some power Paul can't understand, Beloved seduces him. He wasn't seduced by her beauty, he was compelled by the intensity of—of what?—her ravenous need to grab all the life she'd been deprived of, her two-year-old mind in the body of a twenty-year-old woman, her need to exact a price from her mother . . . and her greedy love of her mother.

Paul didn't want it, didn't enjoy it, couldn't have resisted it—but he did it—so he tells Sethe he slept with Beloved and asks Sethe to have his child. While she's thinking it over, a man named Stamp Paid (a well-meaning busybody in this situation, a sadly heroic man in others) shows Paul a newspaper article about Sethe killing her child. Paul confronts Sethe; she explains how entirely she was motivated by love. Paul, whose survival strategy is to love everything "just a little bit," tells Sethe that her love is "too thick." It's a discussion between people who disagree but care deeply for each other until Paul D says, "You got two feet, Sethe, not four." That language was too close to Schoolteacher's despicable lists of animal and human "characteristics" for Sethe to bear, and Paul D knew it as soon as he said it. He leaves; she's determined not to give a damn.

Sethe can't bear the idea that anyone might feel sorry for her, so she takes Denver and Beloved ice skating on the frozen creek. They have a great time, laughing, tumbling across the ice. Back home, over a fire and warm milk, something clicks. Sethe realizes that Beloved is her dead baby and spends her savings on fancy clothes and food to appease Beloved. Driven by some combination of revenge and love, Beloved becomes insatiable and begins draining the life out of Sethe. They run out of money so Denver goes looking for work. A few of their neighbors give food and help, but by that time Beloved has nearly destroyed Sethe, and everyone knows it. Thirty women, the townspeople who had avoided her like the plague for years, come to 124 to help Sethe get rid of Beloved. They join forces and sing the little monster out of Sethe's life! (That bothers some people, but I'm not one of them.) Meanwhile, Mr. Bodwin (an honorable old white guy who opposed slavery and owns 124, but has gone a bit senile in the last few years) comes riding up on a horse, wearing a black hat (Bodwin, not the horse). Sethe, semi-cracked, but spiritually given a second chance, thinks Bodwin is the evil Schoolteacher and tries to terminate him with an icepick. Denver and another woman stop her; Beloved seems to be gone for good, and Paul D wants to try making a life with Sethe again. When Sethe is safe and subdued and they are sure that all is well, Paul D and Stamp Paid begin to laugh:

> "Every time a whiteman come to the door she got to kill somebody?"
> "For all she know, the man could be coming for the rent."
> "Good thing they don't deliver mail out this way."

. . . That covers most of the factual events but barely touches the spiritual ones.

## Toni Morrison Talks about *Beloved*

Elise Washington opens her October 1987 interview of Toni Morrison for *Essence* with a perfect question: "If you were writing the book-jacket copy for *Beloved*, how would you describe it?"

"If I could understand it in a hundred words or less," TM replied, "I probably wouldn't have written the book." What follows is a sampling of her remarks:

≈≈≈≈≈≈≈≈≈≈≈≈≈≈≈≈≈≈≈≈≈≈≈≈≈≈≈≈≈≈≈≈≈≈≈≈≈≈≈≈≈≈≈

In hindsight, I think what's important about it is the process by which we construct and deconstruct reality in order to be able to function in it. I'm trying to explore how a people—in this case one individual or a small group of individuals—absorbs and rejects information on a very personal level about something [slavery] that is undigestible and unabsorbable, completely. . . .

Those people could not live without value. They had prices, but no value in the white world, so they made their own, and they decided what was valuable. It was usually . . . something they were doing for somebody else. Nobody in the novel, no adult Black person, survives by self-regard, narcissism, selfishness. They took the sense of community for granted. It never occurred to them they could live outside it. . . .

Black people live all over the world and in all sorts of neighborhoods, but when they think about comfort and joy, they think about one another. That is the vestige of the days when we thought about staying alive, when we thought about one another. In some ways those were the most complicated of times, in some ways they were not. Now people choose their identities. Now people choose to be Black. They used to be born Black. That's not true anymore.

### TM tells Gail Caldwell

What was on my mind was the way in which women are so vulnerable to displacing themselves, into something other than themselves. . . .

The past, until you confront it, until you live through it, keeps coming back in other forms. The shapes redesign themselves in other constellations, until you get a chance to play it over again. . . .

≈≈≈≈≈≈≈≈≈≈≈≈≈≈≈≈≈≈≈≈≈≈≈≈≈≈≈≈≈≈≈≈≈≈≈≈≈

If you have trouble believing that an author can be the worst judge of her own work—and many people do—Toni Morrison's reaction to her own novel is proof positive.

TM had conceived of the novel as a three-volume work, but after working on the book for three years, she became seriously blocked, and gave the stalled partial manuscript to her editor Bob Gottlieb, with apologies for her "failure."

> I had decided that I was never going to meet the deadline, and I would just have to live with it. But I gave Bob what I had, and said, "I'm sorry, because I really and truly have only a third of a book."
>
> And he read it and said, "Whatever else you're doing, do it, but this is a book." I said, "Are you sure?"
>
> —to Gail Caldwell

Morrison couldn't believe it. She kept asking Gottlieb if he was sure that it was really a book. She had given him *Beloved,* the entire book, except for the page-and-a-half coda at the end.

## What Did the Critics Say?

*Beloved* got spectacular reviews—

> [In this] magnificent novel, . . . [a slave's] interior life is re-created with a moving intensity no novelist has even approached before. . . . The splintered,

piecemeal revelation of the past is one of the technical wonders of Morrison's narrative. We gradually understand that this isn't storytelling but the intricate exploration of trauma. . . . The flood of daylight that ends the book is overpowering. I think we have a masterpiece on our hands here: difficult, sometimes lushly overwritten, but profoundly imagined and carried out with burning fervor.

—Walter Clemons, *Newsweek*

The flesh-and-blood presence of Beloved roils the novel's intense, realistic surface. This young woman may not actually be Sethe's reincarnated daughter, but no other explanation of her identity is provided. Her symbolic significance is confusing: she seems to represent both Sethe's guilt and redemption. . . . In the end, the implausibilities in Beloved may matter less than the fact that Sethe believes them. . . . [S]he sees no distinction between the supernatural and the equally surreal facts of her own life. Morrison's heroine is hard to understand and to forget.

—Paul Gray, *Time*

Ms. Morrison's versatility and technical and emotional range appear to know no bounds. . . . "Beloved" is written in an antiminimalistic prose that is by turns rich, graceful, eccentric, rough, lyrical, sinuous, colloquial and very much to the point. . . . In this book, the other world exists and magic works, and the prose is up to it. If you can believe page one—and Ms. Morrison's verbal authority compels belief—you're hooked on the rest of the book.

—Margaret Atwood, *New York Times Book Review*

A life-affirming novel . . . strong enough to break your heart.

—Gail Caldwell, *Boston Globe*

*Beloved* belongs on the highest shelf of our literature even if half a dozen canonized Wonder Bread Boys have to be elbowed off. . . . Without *Beloved*, our imagination of America had a heart-sized hole in it big enough to die from.

—John Leonard, *Nation*

One of the few downright hostile reviews of *Beloved* was written by Stanley Crouch for the *New Republic.* Stanley might have made a few good points if his review hadn't been so nasty and personal—it seemed to be directed less at Morrison's novel than at Toni Morrison, herself.

> It is designed to . . . make sure that the vision of black woman as the most scorned and rebuked of the victims doesn't weaken. Yet perhaps it is best understood by its italicized inscription: "Sixty Million and more." Morrison recently told *Newsweek* that the reference was to all the captured Africans who died coming across the Atlantic. But sixty is ten times six, of course. That is very important to remember. For *Beloved,* above all else, is a blackface holocaust novel.

"Sixty million and more." In an interview with Toni Morrison in 1989, Bonnie Angelo challenges TM's number vigorously ("is this proved historically?"), but I'll give you ten-to-one odds that she's never questioned the number (or lack of one) in our own history books. Allowing white scholars to define slavery is exactly as fair, reasonable, and humane as allowing the Nazis to define the Holocaust. No country, America included, is honest about its crimes until the victims force an honest accounting.

Those of you who are unfamiliar with the research and logic behind those numbers, see S. E. Anderson's fine, truthful book, *The Black Holocaust for Beginners.*

The article continues in the same vein. Brutal and very personal. I know quite a few people who don't love Stanley Crouch. I don't know much about him (a few articles, a couple TV shows) but he strikes me as real smart. And he seems to have courage. But to accuse Morrison of writing "a blackface holocaust novel." That strikes me as so intentionally hurtful that I wonder if there's some evil personal stuff going on between them. (I'm not up-to-date on literary gossip.) If Crouch disagreed with TM's numbers, if he thought 60 million was inaccurate, then dispute the numbers in a fair way without the accompanying kicks in the stomach. He ignores her argument and attacks her. (*Argumentum ad wominem . . . ?*) (Bad timing; can't help it, it's genetic.)

Mr. Crouch wasn't the only person who zeroed in on TM's dedication. Maybe we should talk about that.

## THE DEDICATION

To be perfectly blunt about it, I've never heard of a novel that got so much flak over its dedication: "Sixty million and more." People who never questioned a thing in their lives, suddenly getting self-righteous and demanding PROOF. Letters, reviews, interviews. In 1989, Bonnie Angelo interviewed Toni Morrison for *Time*. Ms. Angelo is probably a very nice lady, but her interview with TM was so out of synch with everything Toni Morrison "stands for" (Morrison is one of the few writers who does stand for something) that they seem to have each other by the throat on the first page. They politely knock heads over a few issues, drop the politeness when they discuss young women having babies, then, Bonnie Angelo asks TM about the dedication . . . sort of like she's been saving it up:

> **Bonnie Angelo:** *Beloved* is dedicated to the 60 million who died as a result of slavery. A staggering number—is this proved historically?
>
> **"Evander" Morrison:** Some historians told me 200 million died. The smallest number I got from anybody was 60 million. There were travel accounts of people who were in the Congo—that's a wide river—saying, "We could not get the boat through the river, it was choked with bodies." That's like a logjam. A lot of people died. Half of them died in those ships.

*Beloved* shows us how black Americans repress and deny the experience of slavery. White America represses and denies slavery by underreporting the numbers, by refusing to fund research that would unrepress those numbers, and by acting as if slavery was just a job that people of African descent had a natural aptitude for. I commissioned and edited S. E. Anderson's book (see sidebar on previous page). Sixty million is very possible.

## FROM THEM (THROUGH HER) TO US

*Beloved* is generally considered Toni Morrison's most difficult book, but in some ways it's actually the most straightforward of all her novels. You can't read it without knowing that it's "about" slavery as a personal experience (slavery with a small *s*), not Slavery-the-institution. And you can't miss the fact that it's an intimate, incredibly personal novel from her to us. Or, from them, through her, to us. The feeling you get when you read *Beloved* is that Toni Morrison couldn't have written that book—nobody could—she must've channeled it. (And I don't even believe in that stuff.)

Whether by magic or mysticism or extraordinary use of ordinary faculties (like thought and imagination), Toni Morrison has written a novel so authentic that it feels as if she must have brought it back from the "other side." It's hard to believe that the slaves themselves didn't whisper it in her ear. (Of course, in one way or the other, they did.)

*Beloved* is so moving that a few carried-away critics thought that Morrison's novel made them "experience slavery." Please, let's don't be so self-involved that we imagine that reading about slavery is the same as living it. That would be an insult to Toni Morrison and to the people she writes about. The most a novel can hope to achieve is to render its characters so convincingly that we put some part of ourselves in their place, feel some of what they feel. If you were a slave, what would they do to your body, mind, spirit, soul, memory? What would they do to your parents, friends, children? What would it cost you to survive that, or to stand by and watch it? What would you have to amputate to get through the day?—your pride, your innocence, your ability to love or to see colors or to make logical connections? And if they suddenly give you— give me—my freedom, how do I go about becoming my real self when I have no idea what my real self is? Or what freedom is? Or who *they* are?

*Beloved* is also about love—above all, the unbounded love of a mother for her children. Don't think you can let yourself off the hook just because you're a man. Toni Morrison is talking to all of us. If you have the guts, she is offering you the chance to transcend gender, geography, time—the limits of your own everything—and be Sethe, a woman who is strong and resourceful and who loves her children so much that she is willing to risk anything, including the wrath of God, to save them from slavery. She manages to "save" only one of her children before she is restrained. She rejects the censure of her neighbors and refuses to feel guilt before God. There is only one person in the world she is answerable to. You are Sethe: The child you killed out of love wants to have a word with you . . .

*Beloved* is about all of that and more. But when you read it, be prepared.

What I thought over and over again as I read *Beloved* was, "How could she do it? Toni Morrison must have gone through so much pain to write this book. How could she do it?"

. . . and how could they survive it? They survive it like most people survive the truly unbearable events of their lives: by repressing it. Everyone in the novel believes that the way to freedom lies in forgetting the past. Baby Suggs, a character so glorious—a *person* so glorious—that her spiritual exhaustion (for me) was an event every bit as shattering as Sethe's killing of her child, goes so far as to forbid any talk of slavery. If survival does depend on forgetting, then they're all doomed, because the past keeps leaking through. Through the different voices and memories, including Sethe's mother, a survivor of the Middle Passage, we get a taste of slavery from the viewpoint of its victims.

Margaret Atwood expresses, with compassion and understanding, slavery's effect on the family in abstract terms: "Above all, it [slavery] is seen as one of the most viciously anti-family institutions human beings have ever devised."

Baby Suggs's life tells you what the abstraction means to its victims:

> Anybody Baby Suggs knew, let alone loved, who hadn't been run off or been hanged, got rented out, loaned out, bought up, brought back . . . mortgaged, won, stolen or seized.

Some writers think books are more important than life; I'm not one of them, so it seems shallow to switch from a discussion of the horrors of slavery to rapping about the subtleties of *Beloved* as a book. But don't let's kid ourselves: The fact that it's about slavery doesn't make *Beloved* a great book. There are dozens of lousy books on every subject, including slavery. But *Beloved* is so fine on so many different levels that we're going to begin by pulling away from it so that we can see the whole thing at once . . .

## A Look at the Overall Structure

The earth looks, feels, and IS a lot different if you're stuck in traffic in Times Square than if you are looking at it from atop the Empire State Building or standing on the moon. To understand anything, from the earth to a novel, you have to find a way to pull back from it far enough to see its overall shape and structure. It takes a bit of work to uncover the structure of a novel, but when a novel's rhythm feels as elegant as *Beloved*'s, it's exciting to discover how it got that way and to see what surprises it reveals.

**B** = the page the chapter Begins on;

**L** = Length of the Chapter;

(page numbers refer to Plume paperback)

### Part One

| B | L | Ch | *Opening Words of Chapter* |
|---|---|----|----------------------------|
| 3 | 1 | 1 | 124 was spiteful. |
| 20 | 9 | 2 | Not quite in a hurry |
| 28 | 15 | 3 | Denver's secrets were sweet. |
| 43 | 7 | 4 | Pleasantly troubled |
| 50 | 8 | 5 | A fully dressed woman |
| 57 | 8 | 6 | Rainwater held on |
| 64 | 10 | 7 | Beloved was shining |
| 74 | 12 | 8 | Upstairs Beloved was dancing |
| 86 | 20 | 9 | It was time to lay it all down |
| 106 | 8 | 10 | Out of sight |
| 114 | 4 | 11 | She moved him |
| 118 | 7 | 12 | To go back |

| B | L | Ch | *Opening Words of Chapter* |
|---|---|----|---------------------------|
| 125 | 8 | 13 | The last of the Sweet Home men |
| 133 | 2 | 14 | Denver finished washing the dishes |
| 135 | 13 | 15 | In the back of Baby Suggs's mind |
| 148 | 6 | 16 | When the four horsemen came |
| 154 | 6 | 17 | That ain't her mouth. |
| 159 | 6 | 18 | "She was crawling already . . ." |

### Part Two

| B | L | Ch | *Opening Words of Chapter* |
|---|---|----|---------------------------|
| 169 | 31 | 19 | 124 was loud. |
| 200 | 5 | 20 | Beloved, she my daughter. |
| 205 | 5 | 21 | Beloved is my sister. |
| 210 | 4 | 22 | I am Beloved and she is mine. I see |
| 214 | 4 | 23 | I am Beloved and she is mine. Sethe |
| 218 | 12 | 24 | It was a tiny church |
| 230 | 5 | 25 | "Howdy." |

### Part Three

| B | L | Ch | *Opening Words of Chapter* |
|---|---|----|---------------------------|
| 239 | 24 | 26 | 124 was quiet. |
| 263 | 9 | 27 | Bare feet and chamomile sap. |
| 274 | 2 | 28 | There is a loneliness |

Several things are immediately apparent: the novel has a pyramid shape—large bottom (beginning), medium middle, small top; the number of chapters (28) corresponds to the lunar/menstrual cycle (it IS a book about women); each of the three parts begins with a long chapter describing the state of the house

"124," as it goes from "spiteful" to "loud" to "quiet"; many of the chapters are very short (two to seven pages) for a Toni Morrison novel.

Look at it: SEE the novel as if it were a painting or a piece of sculpture; take in its shape, structure, design. • Beloved first comes into the novel in Chapter 5. • Sethe doesn't fully realize that Beloved is her daughter until Chapter 19, two-thirds of the way into the book. (Feel the rhythm of WHEN things happen.)

(Some of the things you come up with, interesting as they seem, are probably coincidental. Part One has *18* chapters, Part Two has *7,* Part Three has *3:* put them together, you get 1873, the year the novel opens and most of the present-tense action takes place.

Chapters 20, 21, 22, and 23 are the only difficult part of the book; we'll discuss them in a minute . . . but notice where they're placed . . . and how short they are.

You can actually SEE the relationship of each Part to the Whole. You can see that Part One is nearly twice as long as Parts Two and Three combined. And if you've read the novel, you may have noticed that the language in Part One was much more restrained than we've come to expect from Toni Morrison. Toward the end of Part One, as we near the climactic scene, the language gets more expansive. By the time TM gets to the four stream-of-consciousness chapters in Part Two (Chaps. 20–23), we're already 200 pages into the novel—so, with perfect writerly instincts, she knows she can dynamite the language without scaring off less-experienced readers. Even then, she doesn't test your patience by making those sections long. The first two are five pages each, the second two are four pages. Those four chapters are what writers call stream-of-consciousness or interior monologue—a writer's attempt to reproduce the process of thinking. (As if you spoke your uncensored thoughts into a tape recorder). The four chapters break down like this:

*Chapter 20:* "Beloved, she my daughter." is Sethe's stream-of-consciousness.

*Chapter 21:* "Beloved is my sister." is Denver's stream-of-consciousness.

*Chapter 22:* "I am Beloved and she is mine. I see . . ." is Beloved's "Middle Passage" stream-of-consciousness.

*Chapter 23:* "I am Beloved and she is mine. Sethe . . ." is Beloved's stream-of-consciousness & poetic dialogue.

# $E$ACH OF THE FOUR CHAPTERS, IN MORE DETAIL . . . ≈≈≈≈≈≈≈

*Chapter 20:* Beloved, she my daughter.
Sethe's stream-of-consciousness: Sethe ruminates on being a mother and on her own mother, Ma'am, who survived the Middle Passage and was forced to nurse white children; Sethe's mind wanders through the past: telling Mrs. Garner that the nephews violated her breasts, Mrs. Garner, a helpless invalid, couldn't do anything; Sethe, above all, is obsessed with Beloved,

*Chapter 21:* Beloved is my sister.
Denver's stream-of-consciousness: Denver recollects her brothers' fears that their mother might kill them like she killed Beloved; Denver admits that she's a recluse, always on the alert that her mother might kill her, too; her mission is to protect Beloved from their mother.

*Chapter 22:* I am Beloved and she is mine. I see . . .
Beloved's "Middle Passage" stream-of-consciousness: This is by far the most difficult Chapter—sentences without punctuation and phrases that seem to be elbowing each other out of the way—but even it isn't difficult if you relax and don't exactly read it, but treat it as if it were a piece of music: NOT intended to transmit "word" information, but meant to evoke a mood, to give voice, pay homage, and honor the millions of Africans killed during the Middle Passage. In death, Beloved merged with her own dead ancestors in an underwater nightmare of the Collective Unconscious. One reason it isn't easy reading is that, to TM's credit, she wouldn't take the easy way and let Beloved have a grown-up mind even for a few pages. She was a two-year-old child at the bottom of the ocean in boats more crowded than being in a coffin. Beloved, despite death, despite her spirit cast into the ocean and her soul left to wander among the souls of her dead ancestors—despite all that, she longs for life and for her mother: "she is my face smiling at me."

   (Reader—don't be afraid of this piece. Let it be what it is to you.)

*Chapter 23:* "I am Beloved and she is mine. Sethe . . ."
Beloved's stream-of-consciousness & poetic dialogue: This is an easier stream-of-consciousness than the preceding one. Then it turns into a kind of obsessive, possessive poetic dialogue (imaginary, I think) between Sethe and Beloved, then Denver and Beloved, then all three, in which they seem to want to possess each other. The trio for three voices ends as many curses, incantations, and prayers end—repeated three times: "You are mine. You are mine. You are mine."

≈≈≈≈≈≈≈≈≈≈≈≈≈≈≈≈≈≈≈≈≈≈≈≈≈≈≈≈≈≈≈≈≈≈≈≈≈≈≈≈≈≈≈

The narrative structure of *Beloved* is downright beautiful. In Chapter 8, there's a seamless transition from Denver and Beloved telling a story to the story actually happening. In Chapter 9, an elegant transition from Ella's point-of-view to Sethe's. In Chapter 16, TM passes the point-of-view, amazingly, brilliantly, to the white slave catchers. Again and again, consciousness is passed from person to person like a baton in a relay race. The narrative structure is complex and subtle but you can always feel the logic in the shifts.

The language in TM's other books is beautiful, but it is often larger than the characters. The language in *Beloved* is powerful without overwhelming its people. It is as if there were no author, no ego, no anything between the people in the book and us. (That changes somewhat toward the end of the book.)

---

### Symbols & Motifs in *Beloved*

- **milk** = motherhood
- **water** = divides earth from afterlife
- **river** = divides freedom & slavery
- **124** (the House Number) is repeated like a motif or mantra; 1+2+4 = 7; 7 is a key number in religion and myth
- **red** = Beloved's signature color; as a spirit "a pool of red undulating light"
- **colors** = the Inability to see them signifies a closing off of the senses and a withdrawal of the self
- **corn** = female genitalia ("how loose the [corn] silk")
- **fingers & hands** = healing, comforting
- **breastfeeding** = comforting, caring
- **Sweet Home** = both Eden & Hell; parody of "My Old Kentucky Home"
- **shadows** = hidden truths
- **Baby Suggs** = Earth Mother, nurturer
- **unlined hands** = signifies a ghost

*continued*

---

## Symbols & Motifs in *Beloved*

- Sethe's lack of bladder control when she sees Beloved = before a woman gives birth, her "water breaks"

- Sethe's "diamonds" = crystal earrings, a wedding present from Mrs. Garner

- **heart** = nurturing, the "prize"

- **way station** = a safe place for a runaway slave (or a wandering spirit)

- **Paul D's journey** = Odysseus' journey (from Homer's epic, *The Odyssey*)

- **tobacco tin** = metaphor for where Paul D kept bad memories; the lid flies off when he has sex with Beloved

- **Four Horsemen** = schoolteacher, one nephew, a slave catcher, and a sheriff; Four Horsemen of the Apocalypse—famine, war, pestilence, & death

- **hubris** = (pride, arrogance) classical theme; a trait of the Tragic Heroine

- **"the men without skin"** (Middle Passage stream-of-consciousness) = white men

---

## LET ME COUNT THE WAYS

More than any of her other novels, *Beloved* holds together as a Eurocentric novel. She didn't curve off the track onto beautiful but irrelevant meanders. She didn't people *Beloved* with fascinating characters the novel didn't need. TM's earlier books often seemed to be made of pieces that could be moved, removed, or shifted from book to book without greatly changing the book's character. (TM herself describes BLUEST EYE and SULA as "pieces of a broken mirror.") But in *Beloved,* everything connects, everything fits—each of the parts contributes to the whole. In other books, her causes often didn't seem (to me) to be connected to their effects. But in *Beloved* the "chain of causality" is always convincing, and the suspense never seems forced or artificially prolonged.

Do I have any reservations about the book?

Sure. I think that almost anyone who hears that a woman has killed her children rather than let them be taken into slavery understands why the woman did it. It has that sense of instant logic, that Greek-tragedy-rightness about it. Not only doesn't it need explanation, but explanation diminishes it. For me, the more TM "explained" the event, or the more specific she made Sethe's motives, the weaker it got. The everyday events of slavery were enough to push Sethe—or anyone—over the edge. TM started out with a ready-made Greek tragedy . . . and then she tried to *turn it* into a Greek tragedy. And when the novel (or TM), in effect, took Sethe to task for killing her child, I felt like we were reasoning with Medea (now listen, honey, this time, when Jason walks in the door, whack him, not the children); but since we know that her actions were perfect, we are the crazy ones. And if we are allowed to chastise Sethe for killing her child, are we suggesting that we have moral reservations about the women killing their own children that had been fathered by white rapists? (Yeah, baby, we're going to have moral reservations about it, but we're gonna do it anyway.)

I also loved the toned-down writing in the first half of the book . . . It put the spotlight on the people instead of on the writing. It was as if, in the second half of the novel, TM just couldn't restrain her pencil any longer. There was an enormous air of "implied respect" for the characters in the first half of the book precisely because it was written by Toni Morrison. By underwriting that first half, the best line-to-line writer in the universe was saying, in effect, What they are going through is more important than my words.

My Bottom Line feeling about *Beloved* . . . ?

If you put all of my complaints together and weigh them against what is wonderful about the novel, they would amount to something approximately as important as if I said, "I think the Atlantic Ocean would be even better if you removed five tablespoons of water from it." Whatever I thought Toni Morrison might have done differently in *Beloved,* the novel exactly as it is could not have moved me more. I reached MY limits, not its.

I keep realizing new ways in which the book took us in its arms and put us where it wanted us. Like: The fact that we could all understand the pure clear logic of a woman murdering her own child rather than let it be a slave makes us co-conspirators, collaborators, participants. The first item on Toni Morrison's list of characteristics for her African-American novel is to make the readers participants. She got us. At last count, Toni Morrison had actualized all of the hoped-for characteristics of her African-American novel except two:

- An obligation to bear witness
- A novel that would take her people through the pain and denial of their racially haunted history to a healing zone

What I find amazing is that *Beloved* seems to have been—or actually was—designed consciously and intentionally exactly in line with those goals, but the novel itself doesn't feel stiff or artificial or consciously manipulated at all. It feels like it was born, not written!

Way back in Toni Morrison's bio, I copped an attitude over the fact that black writers and critics muscled the gents who give the awards. I'm not crazy about intimidation, even when you're dealing with jerks, but I wrote that part before I read *Beloved.* Now that I've read it, I think you'd have to be dead for at least a week to miss the power of *Beloved.* John Leonard wrote (facetiously, I hope) that the main reason the naysayers gave for not loving *Beloved* was the Ghost. (Hey, maybe they dissed *Hamlet,* too?)

I've read that there are people who don't love *Beloved* because they don't believe in ghosts. That strikes me as so blind to the fact of what books do that it's on the same level of irrelevance as saying, "I don't like your book because I don't believe that twenty people can fit inside a novel that's 5″ × 7″. Okay, okay . . . but what do you do with a ghost when you don't believe in ghosts? Do you, as they say, "suspend your judgment"? Must you accept da Ghost as literally real as TM says? In regard to the ghost, as with many other things, Toni Morrison tends to get a bit too managerial, almost to the point of suggesting that if you don't take the ghost as literally real then you've misread the novel. But when a person writes with as much conviction as Toni Morrison wrote *Beloved,* they almost have to believe it! (Don't you just know that every time Edgar Allen Poe wrote the word "Nevermore," he was peeing his pants.) It's a free country: let *her* believe the Ghost is certified and *you* believe whatever you want.

I don't understand why anyone would make a fuss over the ghost. It's a character in a novel. The slave mother killing her child is monumental. The ghost is a petite event compared to that.

. . . a woman kills her baby. More than anything in life, she wants to talk to the baby, to explain, to accept with love whatever punishment the baby thinks she deserves. The baby, murdered at the age of two, doesn't understand why she isn't alive; she is pretty sure her mother loved her but then why did her mother make her not alive? Even dead, she wants her mother, wants life, wants her mother's love, just wants . . .

If anything could turn thought into matter, wouldn't it be that?

You don't judge a book like *Beloved.*

It judges you.

Let us end this chapter with some of the most life-affirming word music ever written.

Baby Suggs, Sethe's mother-in-law, old and gimpy, wonders at first why her son had worked his brains out to buy her freedom. She couldn't imagine what good it could be or what she was going to do with it . . . until she experiences it.

When she experiences it, she becomes Holy.

She gathers her people in the field and says things that make them, and us, Holy:

> She did not tell them to clean up their lives or to go and sin no more. She did not tell them they were the blessed of the earth, its inheriting meek or its glorybound pure.
>
> She told them that the only grace they could have was the grace they could imagine. That if they could not see it, they would not have it.
>
> "Here," she said, "in this here place, we flesh; flesh that weeps, laughs; flesh that dances on bare feet in grass. Love it. Love it hard. Yonder they do not love your flesh. They despise it. They don't love your eyes; they'd just as soon pick em out. No more do they love the skin on your back. Yonder they flay it. And O my people they do not love your hands. Those they only use, tie, bind, chop off and leave empty. Love your hands! Love them. Raise them up and kiss them. Touch others with them, pat them together, stroke them on your face 'cause they don't love that either. You got to love it, you! And no, they ain't in love with your mouth. Yonder, out there, they will see it broken and break it again. What you say out of it they will not heed. What you scream from it they do not hear. What you put into it to nourish your body they will snatch away and give you leavins instead. No, they don't love

your mouth. You got to love it. This is flesh I'm talking about here. Flesh that needs to be loved. Feet that need to rest and to dance; backs that need support; shoulders that need arms, strong arms I'm telling you. And O my people, out yonder, hear me, they do not love your neck unloosed and straight. So love your neck; put a hand on it, grace it, stroke it and hold it up. And all your inside parts that they'd just as soon slop for hogs, you got to love them. The dark, dark liver—love it, love it, and the beat and beating heart, love that too. More than eyes or feet. More than lungs that have yet to draw free air. More than your life-holding womb and your live-giving private parts, hear me now, love your heart. For this is the prize." Saying no more, she stood up then and danced with her twisted hip the rest of what her heart had to say while the others opened their mouths and gave her the music. Long notes held until the four-part harmony was perfect enough for their deeply loved flesh.

*After emancipation . . . all those people who had been slaves, they needed the music more than ever now; it was like they were trying to find out in this music what they were supposed to do with this freedom. . . .*

*[I]t wasn't just white people the music had to reach to, nor even to their own people, but straight out to life, and to what a man does with his life when it finally is his.*

SIDNEY BECHET, *TREAT IT GENTLE* (HIS AUTOBIOGRAPHY)

# JAZZ
## *(1992)*

When Toni Morrison first conceived *Beloved,* she thought of it as Part One of a "triptych"—a novel with three independent sections that took place in three different times. The second part of the trio was to be set in 1920s Harlem, but Morrison was having trouble finishing it, so, as we know, she gave the "unfinished" manuscript to her editor at Knopf Bob Gottlieb with apologies for her "failure." Gottlieb read the section about Sethe and Beloved, realized that it was a masterpiece, published it as *Beloved,* and sent TM home to await the Pulitzer Prize and other signs of radical acclaim.

Among other things, that meant that Toni Morrison had to face the reality that what she'd thought was a middle—the book about Harlem in the 1920s—was actually a beginning. How had the beginning begun? A few years before she thought of writing *Beloved,* Toni Morrison had seen *The Harlem Book of the Dead,* a collection of photographs of dead black New Yorkers taken by James Van Der Zee in the 1920s. It was the fashion of the day to dress your loved ones in their fanciest threads and take pictures of them lying elegantly in their coffins or being cradled lovingly in your arms. One photo especially intrigued Toni Morrison: it was a picture of a dead girl lying in a coffin. The accompanying text explained that the 18-year-old girl had been dancing at a "rent party" when she suddenly slumped over. Her friends rushed to help her, and seeing blood streaming out of her, realized that she must have been shot.

"What happened to you?" her friends asked.

The girl knew that her jealous ex-boyfriend had shot her but she loved him enough to want him to get away. So she said to her friends, "I'll tell you to-morrow." And she died.

## Historical Background

In 1918, when "The War to End All Wars" ended, it seemed like life itself had been given a fresh start. The spirit of rebirth that energized much of the world, held even more promise for black Americans. At the turn of the century, years after Emancipation, freedom without economic opportunity had turned out to be a sick joke. In 1900, 75 percent of America's black population still lived in the South; many of them still worked on cotton plantations, "wage slaves" instead of literal slaves. After the war, factories opened in northern cities, of-fering real jobs. Blacks by the thousands migrated to cities like Detroit, Chicago, and New York. It was a time of great vitality in black American life. Black music and dance so perfectly expressed the national mood that it became known as The Jazz Age.

And Harlem, the intellectual and artistic center of this black awakening, experienced a collective rebirth that became known as the Harlem Renais-sance. Throughout the 1920s, black poetry, art, dance, literature, philosophy, and other expressions of repressed black genius, suddenly burst into full bloom. And jazz, the jewel of African-American art? There might not have been any jazz in Harlem if it weren't for the Southerners. As late as the early 1920s, most New Yorkers (and the North in general) considered Paul Whiteman's and George Gershwin's watered-down versions of watered-down versions of jazz, jazz. (Jazz Muzak!) When the gentlemen from the South—virtually all of jazz's early masters were Southern—brought real jazz and "pre-jazz" (blues, ragtime, stride, etc.) music to Harlem, it was like putting one of those electric zappers on a(n almost) dead man's heart. Just like that, jazz became the heartbeat of the Harlem Renaissance. It was everywhere (you can't get away from your heart-beat). Harlem was becoming one of the major centers of the vibrant new jazz music. Throughout the 1920s downtown New Yorkers flocked to Harlem to hear great jazz artists like Duke Ellington, Fletcher Henderson, Bessie Smith, and Louis Armstrong in the flashy night spots like the legendary Cotton Club. Meanwhile, throughout residential Harlem, the locals held "rent parties," where they hired musicians to play in their own homes and charged a small fee to cover the week's rent. As often as not, those thrown-together little rent parties featured great jazz pianists like "Fats" Waller and James P. Johnson. These people weren't just playing jazz—they were inventing it.

But what about the "regular people," the thousands of Southern blacks who had moved north in search of a better life . . . the ones who had no idea they were living through something fancy like the Harlem Renaissance? *Jazz* is their story.

## JAZZ: THE STORY

Toni Morrison's sixth novel, *Jazz,* ends on the first page:

> Sth, I know that woman. She used to live with a flock of birds on Lenox Avenue. Know her husband, too. He fell for an eighteen-year-old girl with one of those deepdown, spooky loves that made him so sad and happy he shot her just to keep the feeling going. When the woman, her name is Violet, went to the funeral to see the girl and to cut her dead face they threw her to the floor and out of the church. She ran, then, through all that snow, and when she got back to her apartment she took the birds from their cages and set them out the windows to freeze or fly, including the parrot that said, "I love you."

That paragraph raises a dozen questions (but it's gossipy beauty sets the tone of the novel so sweetly that you might want to read it again before we ask them):

Why did a mature married man fall for an 18-year-old girl? Was it because of something lacking in his wife or because of some lack in himself—or was he just another old lech sniffing after some young hips? Why didn't he settle for a roll in the sack instead of falling in "deepdown, spooky love"? Why shoot the girl? Was the murder consistent with his usual behavior or was it a complete deviation? Why does his wife Violet crash the funeral? Why does she try to mess up the girl's face after she's dead? Was Violet a stable person who temporarily lost it because of her husband's affair . . . or was she a little whacked out to begin with? How do the man and wife react after the funeral? How do they cope? (Or do they?) And the young girl's family, friends, neighbors—how do they feel about the killer and his wife? And this 18-year-old girl—what was special about her?

And who is telling us the story? ("Sth" isn't a word, it's a sound—when you do it three times and shake your head No, it means roughly Shame On You; when you do it once, either you're exasperated or you're about to give some "graveyard information.")

*Jazz,* the story of Joe and Violet Trace, is a dark ballad of love and murder and coming to terms with your actions when they're out of whack with the rest of your life. Born, raised, and married in the South, Joe and Violet had come to Harlem so full of hope that even the train they rode from Virginia felt like it was dancing. Twenty years later, their world had shrunk and nothing, including dancing, felt like dancing: Violet was a hairdresser who fell through the cracks in reality and gave the meager remains of her affection to her birds; Joe was a 50-year-old doorbell-ringing cosmetics salesman who remembered the events of love but couldn't quite "catch what it felt like" and suspected that his unruly thoughts were caused by "the sooty music the blind twins were playing."

The year (not counting TM's background checks on all the suspects) is 1926, dead in the eye of Harlem's wake-up call to anyone dumb enough to underestimate black genius. Three hundred years of unsung lovesongs and uncelebrated funerals came screaming out in every imaginable form, from poetry and painting to philosophy and fashion. And above all, music: jazz. The music, the City, the energy create an "appetite," a communal longing and dropping of restraint—DO IT!—whatever it is. Joe Trace meets Dorcas Manfred, a teenager whose parents were killed in the 1919 East St. Louis race riots, and falls crazy in love. The atmosphere in which their story unfolds bears an uncanny resemblance to Duke Ellington's description of his jazz tone poem *Harlem Air Shaft:*

> So much goes on . . . you get the full sense of Harlem in an air shaft. You hear fights, you smell dinner, you hear people making love. You hear the radio. . . . You see your neighbor's laundry. You hear the janitor's dogs. The main upstairs' aerial falls down and breaks your window. You smell coffee. . . . One guy is cooking dried fish and rice and another guy's got a great big turkey.

Guy-with-fish's wife is a terrific cooker but the guy's wife with the turkey is doing a sad job. You hear people praying, fighting, snoring. Jitterbugs are jumping up and down always over you, never below you. . . . I tried to put all that in *Harlem Air Shaft*.

---

## The Major Characters

**Narrator** = unnamed, unidentified?

**Violet Trace** = the main character. She's a hairdresser, married to Joe Trace for 20 years. On the verge of losing her husband and her sanity. When her husband shoots his lover, Violet tries to disfigure the corpse's face.

**Joe Trace** = the "other" main character, Violet's husband, a cosmetics salesman, around 50 years old. (The kind of symbolism I don't love: Joe gave himself the last name Trace because he couldn't find a trace of his mother.)

**Dorcas Manfred** = the girl Joe falls in love with, then kills. She's 18 years old, her parents were killed, she's being raised by her aunt Alice. Her main interest is exploring her sexuality.

**Alice Manfred** = Dorcas' aunt (her mom's sister), fairly well-off; a strict "parent."

**Wild** = Joe Trace's mother.

**Golden Gray** = Joe's father, half-black but white-skinned. When he finds out his father is black, he vows to kill him.

**Rose Dear** = Violet's mother. Overwhelmed by the pressure of trying to support her children, she commits suicide.

**True Bell** = Violet's grandmother, Rose Dear's mother; she takes care of the family after Rose Dear commits suicide.

**Violet's Father** (unnamed) = he drops by once in a while, gives everyone a gift, then splits. He's never around when you need him.

**Malvonne** = Joe and Violet's upstairs neighbor. She lets Joe and Dorcas meet secretly in her apartment (but she feels guilty about it).

*continued*

---

### The Major Characters

**Sweetness** = Malvonne's shifty nephew (he steals people's mail looking for money).

**Acton** = Dorcas's new young boyfriend.

**Felice** = Dorcas's best friend, raised by her grandmother, becomes friends with Joe and Violet.

---

As is usually the case with Toni Morrison novels, the story unfolds, chunk by chunk, toward both future and past. We get a few pages about Violet after the funeral and a few pages about her recent past. Violet had been acting funny for the last year or so, Joe could see that, but everybody acts crazy when they're at home. With his own eyes, Joe could see that Violet always kept it together in public, so as far as he was concerned, she was fine. What neither Violet nor the neighbors had seen fit to mention was that she'd recently had a couple "episodes" in public. Before we can get too worried, TM gives us a couple pages about Joe and Dorcas both before and after the murder, then Joe further back in time. We hear about friends and family, New York and Down South. We learn about Joe's and Violet's background, we gain some insight into why they are the way they are. We learn that Dorcas was neither pretty nor interesting and that Joe is more interesting than he first seemed (a natural woodsman who reinvents himself every few years). We learn that Violet's mother committed suicide because she couldn't bear the pressure of trying to support her children (her grandmother raised her) and that Violet was a strong and assertive young woman until fairly recently, when she began leaking through the cracks.

We meet Alice Manfred, Dorcas's aunt (her mother's sister), a strong, responsible woman who, in her eagerness to be a good parent, raised Dorcas too strictly in an attempt to protect her from the City and the "dirty, get-on-down music" that encouraged everyone to lose control. Not that Dorcas needed much encouraging. She was shallow, self-absorbed, obsessed with her looks, clothing, sex (life's a movie, she's the heroine, the least she can do is be well-dressed for the camera)—a fairly typical 18-year-old girl. But one that Morrison has clearly not made a sympathetic character. (It's interesting now and then to remember that Dorcas might have been the 1920s version of Beloved.) Oddly enough, it's the men in Morrison's novels who are the doomed romantics.

At one point Dorcas urges Joe to leave her, but Joe wouldn't. (Couldn't.) When Dorcas takes up with Acton, a young man around her own age, Joe goes looking for her. He spends five days tracing her movements, not so much in rage or anger; he just kind of switches to the "head" he had when he was a hunter Down South. After he tracks her to a crowded apartment and finds her dancing with her young man, Joe doesn't exactly realize that he's shot her. When he heard the gun go off, he wanted to "catch her before she fell and hurt herself."

Violet's description of her own behavior at the funeral when she tried to slash Dorcas's face is even more disassociated: she watched as "a woman she recognized" elbowed her way through the mourners and raised a knife over the dead girl's face. Later, still, in one of the best scenes in the book, Alice Manfred inexplicably burns a blouse she is ironing. Both women stare at the blouse in disbelief. Then Violet tells Alice how silly she must have looked busting into Dorcas's funeral, fumbling with the knife, "trying to do something bluesy"— and both women burst into healing laughter.

The scenes between Violet and Alice are some of the best parts of the book. Alice doesn't want anything to do with the lunatic wife of the man who killed her niece and Violet wants to learn more about Dorcas so she can hate the girl more precisely. But Violet finds herself beginning to like Dorcas, even to thinking of her as the daughter she might have had, and Alice realizes how much she and Violet have in common.

Dorcas's best friend, Felice, comes into the story, and we are expecting all hell to break loose. The narrator of the story even says she (or he or it) is certain that either Joe or Violet would "kill the other." But nobody kills anybody. Felice had come to tell Joe what really happened with Dorcas to absolve him of some of his guilt—and to tell him to stop grieving over Dorcas because she wasn't worth it. Dorcas had only been wounded in the shoulder and could have easily saved herself, but she was too lazy to either go to the hospital or to let anyone take her. She insisted on going to sleep and bled to death unnecessarily. Felice had planned to just tell the story and leave, but she liked Joe and Violet so much that she told them about herself (she lived with her grandmother and seldom got to see her parents, who were not living in the city) and about her "unusual" friendship with Dorcas. The unusual aspect was that Dorcas was very light-skinned and Felice was very dark—a combination that struck many people, including Felice's grandmother and most of their neighbors and school-mates as incomprehensible. (Even inside the black community, people usually "segregated" themselves by color.)

Before Dorcas died, she'd asked Felice to tell Joe about "the apple," a reference to a story she and Joe shared, implying that Dorcas not only forgave Joe, but considered him her first love. By the time Felice leaves Joe and Violet, it's clear that the three of them have become a family. The book ends with all the right people being happy in a modest way that we modern people probably wouldn't settle for.

Except for the Narrator. The Narrator is upset about jumping to the wrong conclusion in thinking that Felice would be like Dorcas and Joe or Violet would be killed.

### Did the Critics Love Jazz?

In contrast to the overwhelming critical acclaim for *Beloved*, the response to *Jazz* was lukewarm. The book did get some good reviews, even some great ones. John Leonard, in a long, breathless, beautiful rumination on TM's career (1992), said what he always says—Toni Morrison is simply "the best writer working in America." Edna O'Brien, the fine Irish novelist, had some praise for *Jazz,* but she felt that the characters never came to life, that TM had become "bedazzled by her own virtuosity." When all was said and done, too many of the reviews used words like "poetic" and "meta-fiction." One of the most interesting takes on the novel was by Henry Louis Gates, Jr.

Gates, one of the finest critics around, argues ingeniously that Morrison "composed" *Jazz*-the-novel in precisely the way Ellington composed music—for each player's unique sound:

> Like William Faulkner, whose work was the subject of Toni Morrison's master's thesis at Cornell and whose finest work comes to mind again and again as we read through *Jazz,* Morrison's new novel serves to redefine the very possibilities of narrative point of view. Like Duke Ellington, Morrison has

found a way, paradoxically, to create an ensemble of improvised sound out of a composed music. Riffing on these two great geniuses of American literature and music, Toni Morrison has established herself as one of the truly original novelists at work in the world today.

## Morrison: A Book Writing Itself

Toni Morrison told Elissa Schappell and Claudia Brodsky Lacour that she wanted *Jazz* to "be about the people who didn't know they were living in anything as fancy as an 'era.' " She also said that the visual image she had of *Jazz* was of a book "writing itself." She envisioned a book in which some of the notes were "wrong" like a jazz performance. "Sometimes it is wrong because of faulty vision . . . and the characters talk back the way jazz musicians do." Although Morrison had abandoned her original plan to make *Beloved* and *Jazz* part of a trilogy, she did keep some aspects of the plan. One of the most interesting ideas was TM's vision of each of the three books being about a different kind of love carried to the point of outrageous excess.

> *Beloved* was about a mother's love for her children taken to excess.
> *Jazz* was about romantic love, without limits or restraint.
> *Paradise,* would be about . . . let's wait.

## I Guess It's My Turn

Morrison's novel is not about jazz, it aspires to be jazz. At times, you have to damn near nail your shoes to the floor not to dance to it:

> [H]er hand, the one that wasn't holding the glass shaped like a flower, was under the table drumming out the rhythm on the inside of his thigh, his thigh, his thigh, thigh, thigh. . . .

(There's definitely more going on here than meets the eye . . . the eye, the eye, eye, eye.)

We know that TM has described the structure of both *The Bluest Eye* and

*Sula* as being like pieces of a shattered mirror. *Jazz* has a similar structure in the sense that the pieces seem pretty random, but there are a couple things about *Jazz* that give it a distinctly different feel. *The Bluest Eye* was designed around the four seasons, and *Sula* was divided into two parts, each part structured around years (1919–27 and 1937–41). *Jazz* is divided into ten parts that feel very intentional—but if they correspond to anything specific, I sure haven't figured it out. My first expectation (almost too obvious to mention) is that they would correspond in some way to jazz. I know a fair bit about jazz (I wrote a book

> **Structure and Chapter Layout**
>
> **Part 1**—Sth, I know that woman.
> **Part 2**—Or used to.
> **Part 3**—Like that day in July, almost nine years back, . . .
> **Part 4**—The hat, pushed back on her forehead, gave Violet a scatty look.
> **Part 5**—And when spring comes to the City. . . .
> **Part 6**—Risky, I'd say, trying to figure out anybody's state of mind.
> **Part 7**—A thing like that could harm you.
> **Part 8**—There she is. No dancing brothers are in this place. . . .
> **Part 9**—Sweetheart. That's what the weather was called.
> **Part 10**—Pain. I seem to have an affection, a kind of sweettooth for it.

called *Jazz for Beginners*), but I can't find a hard connection between the book's structure and jazz music or jazz history or any particular piece of jazz. The two things that make *Jazz* feel different than TM's other books are that strong feeling of structure with nothing exact to hang it on . . . and the Narrator.

I have so much respect for Toni Morrison after *Beloved* that I want to love *Jazz,* but I don't. What don't I love about it? Although *Jazz*-the-novel in some ways emulates jazz-the-music, most of it doesn't feel like jazz-the-music. Too often the book's pace is languid and mopey; jazz is a fast, summarizing art. Line-to-line, *Sula* was, for me, the most jazzlike of TM's books. It was fast and shifty and full of what jazz critic Whitney Balliet called (in reference to the music, not the novel) "the sound of surprise." And One-Legged Eva was a character right out of a blues song. She spoke in blues lyrics.

If *Jazz*-the-novel is modeled after blues songs, that's a whole 'nuther story. Historically, blues predates jazz. Geographically, blues is country music and jazz is city music (despite great city blues singers like John Lee Hooker). Blues is individual music, jazz is ensemble. But what if, instead of being modeled on Ellington's big band jazz, *Jazz* is seen as a series of blues songs . . . or a blues opera? Barbara Christian, a fine critic and human being who sometimes raps with Toni Morrison, told me that TM said to her, "I write folk operas." (If *Jazz* is a folk opera, it reminds me of the recording of *Porgy and Bess* where Leontyne Price sings all the arias.)

"Real" jazz is generally composed of . . . ? Theme, solo, solo, solo, theme. Call & response. Improvisations—above all, improvisations. Each player (including us, her readers) improvises on—and transforms—the theme. Loving Dorcas, then killing her, is Joe's solo. Disfiguring Dorcas was Violet's solo. (Violet even said it was her attempt to do "something bluesy." It doesn't get much bluesier than that, honey.) Call & response: the parrot: "I love you."

Sidney Bechet's quote that opens this chapter reminds us that jazz, above all, is freedom music. Not only the liberation part of freedom, but the hard questions that Baby Suggs faced in *Beloved:*

> [I]t was like they were trying to find out in this music what they were supposed to do with this freedom . . .
> and [to figure out] what a man does with his life when it finally is his.

When the characters in the novel surprise the Narrator by not doing what she said they were going to do, they are expressing the essence of jazz: Freedom! In *Sula* and *Song of Solomon,* I felt that TM was too controlling, that she forced her characters into a pre-planned ending even if the book had gone off in a new direction. In *Jazz,* the "players" fight back, rebel, assert their freedom. To TM's credit, she "loses" the fight to keep them in "bondage" to the novel's plan. Has any other writer allowed her characters to tell the Narrator—and by implication, the Author—to buzz off, We're doing it our way? Not that I know of.

Is there a singer in this jazz band? Of course there is: Bebop Toni Morrison.

Which brings us to the Narrator.

## THE NARRATOR

As usual with TM, the story is one thing—the way it's told is something altogether else. The most problematic part of the novel by far is the Narrator. My first impulse is to say that the Narrator (or NarratorS) in *Jazz* is one of worst choices I've ever seen a brilliant writer make. My second impulse is to turn that into three "If" statements:

1. IF Toni M wants to draw attention away from her characters and hang a neon sign on the writing—and the writer—that Narrator is the perfect way to do it.
2. IF she wants to make the suspense of how and why Joe, Violet, and Dorcas came to this tragic end take a backseat to the suspense of Who or What that Narrator is—and why He, She, or It is showboating—that Narrator is sure to do it.
3. But if Morrison wants the characters in her novel to feel real and their problems to seem so urgent that they become our problems, that Narrator is a disaster.

My third impulse is to admit with total honesty that it's entirely possible that I have so drastically misunderstood what TM is trying to accomplish in *Jazz* that when I DO understand, I'll change my mind all over the place.

A book, to me, is a serious and beautiful thing. I'm determined to "unmask" the narrator. (But I'm not proud: I'll take all the help I can get.) Jan Furman, in her fine little book *Toni Morrison's Fiction,* feels sure that the Narrator is a woman:

> Slight textual clues and strong intuition points towards the narrator's identity as feminine.

Henry Louis Gates Jr., in his review of *Jazz,* disagrees (but gives himself plenty of wiggle room):

> A final word about Morrison's narrator: despite its revelation of a full and lyrical consciousness, despite its extensive ruminations about its character's consciousness, it remains indeterminate: it is neither male nor female; neither young nor old; neither rich nor poor. It is both and neither.

Plenty of wiggle room! He giveth with the Right hand and taketh away with the Left!

Come on now—are we really such bozos that we honestly can't figure out who or what is telling us the story? Seems impossible, right? But the Narrator seems to keep changing personalities—or "shape shiftin"! Sometimes she/he/it seems like a gossipy neighbor or relative; sometimes the Narrator must be a cat or a small dog who strolls in and out of people's homes through one of those little hinged doors for furry little critters; and sometimes the Narrator is either God or the Dude who Drives the Goodyear Blimp. The epigraph—will that tell us anything? It's from a piece called "Thunder, Perfect Mind," from *The Nag Hammadi,* a collection of Gnostic scriptures from the second or third century found in Egypt in 1945; Gnostics were Christians that valued intuition over faith:

> I am the name of the sound
> and the sound of the name.
> I am the sign of the letter
> and the designation of the division.

Damn! I'm sure glad we cleared that up! (I'd better not comment any further on that. I was the kind of kid who laughed in school at all the wrong times.)

John Leonard (*Nation,* 1992) went through the same boogie I did: he became a detective in search of the Narrator's Identity, worked his way through *The Nag Hammadi,* rejected it, then he concluded that the Narrator was The Book Itself—The Book Its-Friggin'-Self? That sounds damn near as satisfying as eating a photograph of a turkey dinner on Thanksgiving!

When you've worked yourself up to a nice level of frazzlement as I have now—and you want to maintain your RPMs—the one thing you don't want to do is look at her language.

For example the last two paragraphs of the book:

> I envy them [Joe & Violet] their public love. I myself have only known it in secret, shared it in secret and longed, aw longed to show it—to be able to say out loud what they have no need to say at all: *That I have loved only you, surrendered my whole self reckless to you and nobody else. That I want you to love me back and show it to me. That I love the way you hold me, how close you let me be to you. I like your fingers on and on, lifting, turning. I have watched your face for a long time now, and missed your eyes when you went away from me. Talking to you and hearing you answer—that's the kick.*

> But I can't say that aloud; I can't tell anyone that I have been waiting for this all my life and that being chosen to wait is the reason I can. If I were able I'd say it. Say make me, remake me. You are free to do it and I am free to let you because look, look. Look where your hands are. Now.

. . . as I typed Toni Morrison's words onto the page, I was reminded of something my wife said years ago. She was already an accomplished artist, yet she was copying Picasso paintings line for line, color for color. That didn't strike me as a very creative thing to do, so I asked her why she would bother doing it.

"Until you copy them with your own hands," she said, "you can't imagine how beautiful they are."

(I dare you to try it. I dare you to take out your pencil or your pen or your computer and write out those words yourself.)

However . . . I promised you the truth. (No matter how embarrassing it was.)

I am sure that every book reviewer feels this way at some time or other.

It's about time that one of us admitted it.

If I have given you the impression that I understand this book, I apologize.

I understand all the pieces but what they add up to is a mystery to me.

The truth is, I have no idea what this book is about.

I honestly don't have a clue.

*The fathers have eaten sour grapes, and the children's teeth are set on edge.*
—Ezekiel 18:2


*Who controls the past controls the future; who controls the present controls the past.*
—George Orwell, *1984*


# Paradise
## (1998)


After she finished *Jazz* (1992), Toni Morrison settled on an obscure bit of American history for her next novel, *Paradise:* after the Civil War, groups of former slaves headed into Oklahoma and other sparsely populated Western states to set up all-black towns in the wide-open spaces that we usually identify with cowboys! The writing of the novel was marked by interruptions both wonderful (winning the Nobel Prize) and devastating (TM's house burned to the ground, destroying virtually everything of material value to her, including the original manuscripts of many of her books). She was shattered, wondered if there was any point in even trying. Eventually she emerged from her depression and resumed work on her novel.

During a research trip to Brazil, Toni Morrison heard of a convent run by black nuns who took in abandoned children and practiced Catholicism on the first floor and Brazillian Voodoo in the basement. One version of the story (which turned out to be untrue) was that a posse of local men went on a rampage and murdered the nuns.

And the Oklahoma Negros? Two things in particular grabbed Toni Morrison's attention: she came across several newspaper ads seeming to invite black people to join the new communities, but with the enigmatic warning, "Come Prepared or Not at All" . . . and at least one of the black communities in Oklahoma had a most unusual way of organizing their town—their *Paradise*—in terms of color . . .

## PARADISE

The novel opens with these words:

> They shoot the white girl first. With the rest they can take their time. No need to hurry out here. They are seventeen miles from a town which has ninety miles between it and any other. Hiding places will be plentiful in the Convent, but there is time and the day has just begun.
>
> They are nine, over twice the number of the women they are obliged to stampede or kill and they have the paraphernalia for either requirement: rope, a palm leaf cross, handcuffs, Mace and sunglasses, along with clean, handsome guns.

It continues along those lines—stalking, shooting, kicking, blaming, with the utter calm and peace that passeth all understanding that only men who are doing God's work can hide behind. After 16 pages of that, the men corner the women—"God at their side, the men take aim. For Ruby."

## *A*UTHOR'S NOTE ≈≈≈≈≈≈≈≈≈≈≈≈≈≈≈≈≈≈≈≈≈≈≈≈≈≈≈≈

Partway through writing about *Paradise,* I had a "revelation" based largely on the second paragraph quoted above ("They are nine. . . ."), so I have divided this chapter into two sections: *"Paradise:* The Surface" and *"Paradise* Explained: What the Book Is Really About."

If you want to skip the surface and cut to the "EXPLAINED," knock yourself out.

≈≈≈≈≈≈≈≈≈≈≈≈≈≈≈≈≈≈≈≈≈≈≈≈≈≈≈≈≈≈≈≈≈≈≈≈

## PARADISE: THE SURFACE

*Paradise* is essentially two separate books that overlap occasionally until they meet tragically at the end. One book is the story of the all-black town of Ruby, Oklahoma—its citizens, its founders, its reason for being, and the difficulties it has trying to maintain its identity as it heads into the 1970s. The "other" book is the story of the place called the Convent and of the five women who meet and die there. Morrison's novel tells us why the men feel that their Paradise is threatened by the women.

The slaughter that frames the book is set in Oklahoma in 1976. The rest of the novel takes place between 1968 and 1976, with frequent flashbacks going back as far as 1870. The novel is divided into nine sections, each named after a woman. The opening section, like their beloved town, is called Ruby, after Deacon and Steward Morgan's deceased sister. Although Ruby has a population of only 360 people, the novel that tells its story often seems to have more characters than the Bible. That's largely due to the fact that, in order to understand Ruby, Oklahoma (founded in 1950), we have to understand its predecessor, Haven, Oklahoma (founded in 1890).

## The Disallowing

During the 1880s, a group of ex-slaves from Louisiana and Mississippi, led by nine patriarchs, traveled west on foot to settle in the Oklahoma Territory. After great difficulty, they reached Fairly, Oklahoma, an all-black town, and asked its leaders if they could stay. The people of Fairly said "No." Why? The citizens of Fairly were light-skinned blacks; this new band of people were dark. Very dark: they called themselves 8-rocks—men with skin the color of coal from deep in the mines. That rejection, which the outcasts called the Disallowing, became the defining event in their lives:

> Afterwards, the people . . . became a tight band of wayfarers bound by the enormity of what had happened to them. Their horror of whites was convulsive but abstract. They saved the clarity of their hatred for the men who had insulted them in ways too confounding for language. . . .

The outcasts eventually built their own town, which they called Haven.

## Haven and Ruby

Haven was established in 1890, the same year they built the Oven—a communal Oven (always with a capital *O*) where everyone baked their bread. The Oven was also the symbol of their intentional isolation. Through incredibly hard work and true communal spirit (no matter what happened—if your crop failed or you were sick or got hurt—you knew that your neighbors would share everything with you), the community survives, then thrives. By 1905, Haven had 1,000 citizens. Then, in the mid-1930s, young folks began leaving. When World War II started, more young men, including the Morgan twins, Deacon and Steward, joined the Army. When the twins came back to Haven after the war, there was so little left of the town that it seemed like no one cared if they were home or not. So Deek, Steward, their sister Ruby, and 14 other families decided they were going to start from scratch. They dismantled the Oven and headed west to find an isolated place to build their new home. The place they settled on was 90 miles from the nearest town. They named it Ruby, in honor of the twins' sister who died after the journey. The only anything that was nearer than 90 miles was a huge old house 17 miles away that the locals called the Convent.

### The Convent

The Convent, a "big stone house in the middle of nothing," started out as an embezzler's mansion, with statues of naked ladies, doorknobs with nipples, and sexy water faucets. The embezzler was spirited off to jail before he got to use his playhouse, and the place was taken over by nuns and turned into a school for Native American girls. The nuns got rid of some of the porny fixtures, mangled some others, and eventually got used to the rest. By the time that Mavis (the first of the four drop-in "guests" that die in the slaughter) arrives at the Convent (1968), only two people remain: the old, bedridden Mother Superior and a woman who takes care of her, called Connie.

The backgrounds of all the characters appear in bits and pieces throughout the novel. Although each of the nine sections of the novel is named for a female character, the sections are not always confined to that character.

### Mavis

The second section, titled "Mavis," starts out in Maryland in 1968 as Mavis is being interviewed by a local journalist because her newborn twins suffocated in the backseat of her Cadillac. She is pathetic (her husband throws her nightgown over her head when he screws her) (he doesn't make love to her, he *screws* her); she is terrified of her three living children (especially her eleven-year-old daughter Sal); and she is heartbreakingly stupid . . . nothing seems to register. (Toni Morrison, who is generous with the worst of her characters, told Dinitia Smith in the *New York Times,* "That Mavis is stupid! These children die in a Cadillac, and then she goes and says that the twins were the only ones of her children who weren't a trial to her!"

But she loved the hell out of that Cadillac:

> If she could, she would have slept . . . in the back seat, snuggled in the place where the twins had been. . . . She couldn't, of course. Frank told her she better not touch, let alone drive, the Cadillac as long as she lived. So she was surprised as anybody when she stole it.

Mavis steals the Cadillac, drops by to visit her mother, drives toward California. She picks up hitchhikers (girls because they were safe) for company and gas money, including one who collects dog tags from dead soldiers (Mavis had two brothers killed in Vietnam). Mavis runs out of gas a couple miles from the Convent on the outskirts of Ruby, Oklahoma. Instead of panicking or waiting for help like she usually does, Mavis decides that she's sick of being helpless and walks to the Convent.

### Grace

The next chapter, "Grace," is the given name of a sex bomb who called herself Gigi and got off the bus in Ruby a couple years after Mavis stopped by the Convent looking for gas. Gigi is such a Tootsie Roll that the mere sight of her crossing the street stunned all the sidewalk studs into silence. K. D. Morgan, the twins' spineless nephew, happens to be with his pregnant fifteen-year-old girlfriend, Arnette Fleetwood. Arnette, who doesn't take kindly to K. D. gaping at the big-boobed stranger, refers to the lady as a "tramp." K. D. slaps her. And since everyone in town is related to one of the town's Founding Fathers, when a young man of one Family hits a young woman of another Family—especially after he's impregnated her and dismisses it as *her* problem (and his family is as wealthy as hers is bitter)—it's come-together-for-a-meeting time.

We get a good look at the Morgan twins 20 years after the founding of

Ruby. They remember everything, they're the wealthiest brothers in town . . . and they're good ol' capitalists. (They fake a bit of that lofty communal crap like the old-timers had in Haven, but they're too selfish to practice it.) Despite their wealth, they have a problem: Steward and his wife Dovey have come to the stark realization that they can't have children; Deek and his wife Soane had two sons, but they were killed within two weeks of each other in Vietnam. Not only are both families feeling a great sense of emptiness, but in a world based on family—a world of their own making—they had no one to carry on the line. K. D., their sister's son, far from perfect (to say the least), was better than nothing.

At the meeting between the families, we meet the new preacher, Reverend Misner (almost too good-looking to be a preacher), a defender (some say "instigator") of the young, and a spokesman for the totalitarian humanism of the 1960s. We also meet Arnette's overwound brother Jeff Fleetwood (he'd like to kill the Veterans Administration but since that's slightly impossible he has to find someone else to kill). Jeff's free-floating desire to kill somebody is only slightly more urgent than Steward Morgan's. Both men have an itch they're dying to scratch.

You're probably wondering how Gigi the sex bomb wound up at the Convent?

She took a quick walk through town, learned that it didn't have a motel or a diner or anything else that might encourage outsiders to hang around, so she kept an eye out for anyone who'd offer her a ride. Roger Best came by in his ambulance (which doubled as a hearse) and Gigi asked him if the town had a bus or train stop. Roger said he'd drop her at the train stop but first he had to stop at the Convent. At the Convent, Roger picked up the body of the old nun and put it in the hearse (which doubled as an ambulance). Damned if Gigi was going to go riding in a hearse with a dead body. So she stayed in the Convent for a minute to eat a little food and smoke a little grass.

## Seneca

The fourth section, called "Seneca," tells us a lot more about the people of Ruby and the fight over the Oven than it does about Seneca. Seneca, a painfully timid 20 year old, has flashbacks about Kool Aid and Lorna Doones and being abandoned at the age of five. Her abusive boyfriend Eddie had been sent to jail, so Seneca hitchhiked to Wichita to see Eddie's mother. (It's a tiny but powerful part of the book.) Seneca was too shy to hitchhike out of Wichita, so she began "stowing away" in parked trucks and ending up wherever they stopped. When she saw Jeff Fleetwood's crazy wife Sweetie walking along a country road crying, Seneca, in what was probably the first real decision she ever made in her life, jumped out of the truck to comfort her. When Seneca stumbled into the Convent alongside (but not with) Sweetie—roughly three years after Roger dropped Gigi at the Convent for a minute—Gigi and Mavis were still there.

The fight over the Oven? The tension between the young people of Ruby and their elders had been brewing for months. The teenagers hung out at the Oven and blared their radios and threw soda bottles, which was bad enough, but what really ticked the old-timers off was the black fist the kids painted on the Oven. The Oven, though no longer functional, was still the symbolic center of the outcast people and their town. The conflict boiled over when the youngsters demanded the right to change the words on the oven from "Beware the Furrow of His Brow" to "Be the Furrow of His Brow." The furious elders, who would never have contradicted their parents, couldn't understand why these disrespectful teenagers thought they were entitled to an opinion about something they hadn't lifted a finger to build. When Reverend Misner, the liberal new preacher, referred to the words as a "motto," the old fire-breathing Reverend Pulliam flipped out, pointing out that Beware the Furrow of His Brow was "not a suggestion," it was "an order." The kids didn't want to take orders, even from God. They wanted to take part in God's decision-making process themselves—to BE the Furrow of His Brow. In the ensuing argument, Reverend Misner sided with the kids. Steward Morgan, furious, had the last word:

> "If you, any one of you, ignore, change, take away, or add to the words in the mouth of that Oven, I will blow your head off just like you was a hood-eye snake."

The women in *Paradise* are more realistically rendered (and more interesting) than the men, but there are times in the book when all of the good citizens of Ruby, Oklahoma, seem like the Stepford Husbands and Wives. Deek's wife Soane often seems like she's on the verge of some breakthrough or epiphany—the agonized dignity over the death of her sons; the gentle strength with which she faces and handles her husband's affair—but she never quite makes it. Her sister, Steward's wife Dovey, doesn't have much of a role outside of listing Steward's "losses," but she isn't the least bit intimidated by her badass husband. And the only times that Steward comes to life is in his almost boyishly romantic love for his wife: "Sleep without the fragrance of her hair next to him was impossible." (Very touching for such a hardass.)

Meanwhile, Reverend Misner, the liberal young preacher, and Anna Flood, a smart young woman who has returned to Ruby and taken over her father's grocery store, are seriously thinking about getting it on.

We learn more of the history of the founding of Haven and Ruby than any sane person wants to know, but there is one little bit that is so charming. . . . It takes place during the time when the original nine families were checking out towns to see where they might like to live. Some of the towns were disgustingly rich, some of them looked like slave quarters, but in this one particular "prosperous" town, Deek and Steward, who were little kids at the time, sat on a rail fence, watching "nineteen Negro ladies" pose for photographs, their skin "creamy and luminous in the afternoon sun." A few of the younger girls crossed the street and walked "close, so close" to where the boys were sitting:

> The twins did not even look at each other. Without a word they agreed to fall off the railing.

(I defy you *not* to picture these two little kids, bushwhacked by beauty, toppling backward off the rail!)

### Divine

The next section, "Divine," is partly about the fourth "guest" to turn up at the Convent. Her name is Pallas. She hurts so bad she can barely talk. Sixteen years old, wrecked into silence by bad love. (I've already given away more than enough secrets, so I'll leave the rest of her story for you to discover. That won't weaken the focus of the novel, because the stories of each of the Convent women are self-contained.)

**Chronology (Dates Are Approximate)**

**1880s**—158 freedmen, led by the Old Fathers, leave Mississippi and Louisiana to set up a town.

**1889**—79 people, including Big Papa and Big Daddy, get lost outside Fairly, Oklahoma.

**1890**—the Old Fathers establish Haven [in the Oklahoma Territory] • they build the Oven.

**1905**—Haven has grown to 1,000 citizens.

**1910**—Haven has two churches and the All-Citizens Bank • the First Grand Tour: Big Daddy drives around to check out other colored towns.

**1919**—Elder Morgan defends a hooker.

**1920**—Big Daddy travels 65 miles for supplies.

**1922**—the Convent is built.

**1924**—Deacon and Steward Morgan are born.

**1932**—Haven is thriving, unaffected by the Depression • the Second Grand Tour (Ruby, just a baby, stays home).

**1934**—they "dropped to their knees in 1934." Haven is reduced to 500 citizens, then 200, then 80.

**1942**—Deek and Steward enlist in the Army.

**1943**—K.D. Morgan (Coffee Smith) is born.

**1949**—15 families leave Haven to start over.

**1950**—The New Fathers found Ruby. K.D. wins the horse race. Ruby Morgan dies.

**1964**—Soane's baby aborts • Steward and Dovey learn they can't have kids.

**1968**—June: Mavis arrives at the Convent.

**1969**—Scout and Easter Morgan are killed in Vietnam.

**1970**—Rev. Misner comes to Calvary Church• Gigi comes to town and goes to the Convent • the families argue over K.D. and Arnette.

**1973**—the argument over the Oven • Seneca arrives at the Convent.

**1974**—Pallas arrives at the Convent • K.D. and Arnette get married.

**1976**—The men of Ruby attack the Convent.

The section opens in 1974, at the wedding of K.D. and Arnette. Four years have elapsed since K.D. hit Arnette and their families argued. In the meantime, Arnette has gone away to college and returned, and K.D. has hung around the Convent sniffing after Gigi until she dumped him. Although they are to be married by sporty young Reverend Misner, the ceremony opens with a brutal sermon by the old fire-and-brimstoner, Reverend Pulliam, to the effect that, What makes you so arrogant that you think that God is interested in you? After a few beats, both Reverend Misner and Anna Flood realize that Pulliam's accusatory sermon is directed at Misner, who insulted the good people of Ruby with his "namby-pamby sermons of a man who thought teaching was letting children talk as if they had something important to say that the world had not heard and dealt with already." Misner is so rattled that he spends five pages examining his spiritual toothache while he stands motionless, holding up a cross. And the wedding:

> He [K.D.] looked up at the cross Reverend Misner was holding, holding, holding.

But that wasn't the worst thing that happened that day: Soane, Deek's wife, had made the mistake of inviting the Convent women to K. D. and Arnette's wedding reception.

Connie didn't come, but the others did. Mavis, Gigi, Seneca, and Pallas "piled out of the [Cadillac] looking like go-go girls: pink shorts, skimpy tops, see-through skirts. . . ." There was no liquor at the reception, so the Convent girls strolled over to the Oven where the radio was and started into some serious partying. Reverend Pulliam and his wife knew that "fun-obsessed adults" were clear signs that the world was going to hell. "But not here," Reverend Pulliam thought. "Not in Ruby. Not while Senior Pulliam was alive."

Anna, on the other hand, thought the Convent women had saved the day: "Nothing like other

SUSPENSE in a novel is usually created by making us wonder what happens next in the story, but in *Paradise*, Toni Morrison generates discrete little chunks of suspense by making us wonder who each section is named for. In the section called "Grace," she makes us wait until the end to find out that Gigi's real name is Grace (then plays off the word "grace" for a bit of added juice). In the "Seneca" section, TM gives us a long rap on the citizens of Ruby before she even mentions Seneca, and then she messes with our minds for awhile by "inviting" us to confuse Seneca with Sweetie. In the "Divine" section, when TM finally spills the beans about who Divine is—Pallas's boyfriend-stealing mother—we are a wee bit disappointed . . . but later in the novel, TM turns that disappointment into something beautiful.

folks' sins for distraction." Anna also had her own version of the words that should be written on the Oven: Be the Furrow of Her Brow.

≈≈≈≈≈≈≈≈≈≈≈≈≈≈≈≈≈≈≈≈≈≈≈≈≈≈≈≈≈≈≈≈≈≈≈≈≈≈≈≈≈≈

At this point in the book, the chaos of names was so overwhelming that I thought that if there was one thing I should do to help the reader make sense of this novel, it would be to prepare a genealogy, so I stopped reading and spent several hours trying to make sense of all the characters. (As you will see, that turned into a bad joke.)

≈≈≈≈≈≈≈≈≈≈≈≈≈≈≈≈≈≈≈≈≈≈≈≈≈≈≈≈≈≈≈≈≈≈≈≈≈≈≈≈≈≈

Reverend Misner, who hadn't quite finished beating himself up for being snookered by Pulliam, got to the wedding reception just in time to see the Convent women leaving—they'd been thrown out by the "preacher types."

On the ride back to the Convent, Mavis and Gigi get into a fist fight.

As the chapter ends, Mavis is talking to her dead twins.

## Patricia

You've heard of shaggy dog stories? The sixth section, "Patricia," named for Pat Best—a schoolteacher, the daughter of Roger Best (the hearse driver), and the woman who was working on the town's genealogy—is a Shaggy Ancestor Story. Pat had been working on the genealogy for years, borrowing the family Bibles of other founding families, asking questions, scrutinizing gossip for whatever facts it might contain, then constantly adjusting the whole works to accommodate new insights. To anyone like myself who had already had their tolerance for names and relationships exhausted 150 pages ear-

> The reverends disagree on two major points:
>
> **1.** Pulliam believes that God is not interested in you; Misner believes that not only is God interested in you, He is you.
> **2.** Pulliam feels that the cross should not have Jesus on it; Misner believes that a cross with nobody on it makes Christianity just like every other religion in the world.
>
> Misner thinks both points amount to the same thing because he sees Jesus, open arms, inviting us to share everything—His pain and His power.

lier, this was like being caught in a landslide of falling ancestors and unattached nametags. Then Patricia decides that, since people lie about who they have sex with, any genealogy is doomed from the start—so she burns all of her papers! (TM must have been in the Mother of All Reader-Hating Moods when she wrote that chapter!)

In the process of trying to figure out why some of the community's original families (including her own) no longer seemed to be part of the town's "holy families," she realizes the unstated principle behind how people had been ranked in Haven and Ruby since the beginning: skin color. They believed they would be God's chosen people as long as they kept their 8-rock blood untainted. Anyone who mated with a light-skinned person or had light-skinned children had relinquished the racial purity on which their identity was based. "In that case," Patricia thought, "everything that worries them must come from women."

## Consolata

The seventh section is "Consolata." Frankly, I wasn't sure what the word meant. It sounded more like the name of a certain kind of prayer or part of a Good Friday service than a woman's name, but it turned out to be the given name of Connie, the steadfast but uninteresting woman who runs the Convent.

We learn that years earlier, before the nuns came to the Convent, during a previous tour of duty in Brazil, the good sisters had stolen a child from the slums of Rio. They raised Consolata, the stolen child, as if she were one of them. And Consolata came to think of the Mother Superior—the last of the nuns to die—as her own mother. For her first 30 years in the Convent, Consolata devoted herself to God.

Then one day she saw Deek Morgan:

> He was twenty-nine. She was thirty-nine.
> And she lost her mind. Completely.

It's by far the most interesting section in the book—love, lust, instant transformations, fairly unburdened by TM's speeches, or ancestors' genealogies;

Connie meets Deek's twin and his wife and she's even "tricked into raising the dead"—all magic and no realism. In the last few pages of the chapter she undergoes another transformation, becoming a sort of guru of a spiritual girl scout camp:

> "If you have a place . . . that you should be in and somebody who loves you waiting there, then go. If not stay here and follow me. Someone could want to meet you."

## Lone

The eighth section is called "Lone," after Lone DuPres, the 86-year-old midwife and general magic woman who drove out to the Convent in the middle of the night to warn the women but they just "yawned and smiled." The chapter ends with several pages that describe in more detail the slaughter that opened the book.

The last page of the chapter describes either a supernatural occurrence—or somebody's attempt to make it look like one.

The page before that (page 291, Knopf hardcover) describes a tiny bit of Morrison Magic that moved me to tears. (I don't want to say exactly what it is because I don't want to water down the magic for you; I will say only that it made me re-shift the meaning of an entire section from earlier in the book.)

## Save-Marie

The ninth section, "Save-Marie," is the name of one of Jeff and Sweetie Fleetwood's sickly (perhaps deformed or retarded) children. (We're never told what's wrong with them; the implication is that it's the result of inbreeding caused by the group's isolation.)

The situation: Save-Marie's funeral. The chapter expands to sample how each of the characters we've met tells the story of the slaughter of the Convent women—and how the town reacts to it. The story ends with . . . no, let's save that for you to discover.

## How Did the Critics React to *Paradise*?

On the surface, they don't seem to agree on anything—the book opens with, "They shoot the white girl first."—and they don't even agree on who the white girl IS! (You'll learn why in a minute.) On the other hand, they all have the same blind spots, they all jump to the same mistaken conclusions, they all think that what they see on the surface of *Paradise* is what the novel is about . . .

> . . . Pallas, a . . . privileged white girl whose . . . parents have failed her miserably.
>
> —Brooke Allen, *New York Times Book Review*

> . . . Seneca, a white runaway . . .
>
> —Louis Menand, *New Yorker*

Brooke Allen's piece praised the novel—

> *Paradise* . . . is possibly her best work of fiction to date.

> Morrison has brought it all together: the poetry, the emotion, the . . . symbolic plan.

. . . with a couple not-too-serious reservations—

> The male-female dichotomy . . . is a . . . cliché, and Morrison plays it too heavily . . . *Paradise* . . . is not an easy read . . . it requires close scrutiny and observation.

Louis Menand's perceptive piece actually made a virtue of the fact that the novel was a difficult read—

> One reason that these stories are so gripping is that they are hard to understand. The energy we have to expend puzzling out the various pieces and getting them into some kind of satisfactory narrative shape keeps our focus on

the realistic plane of the novel and allows the allegorical machinery to operate more or less hidden from view. The obscurity is deliberate. Morrison has always been careful to make her writing elliptical. Her reason, as she once explained, is that she wants "to provide the places and spaces so that the reader can participate . . . to have the reader *work* with the author in the construction of the book."

David Gates's review in *Newsweek* expressed some serious reservations:

> we're asked to swallow too many contrivances: the cultists' hangout was originally a decadent mansion with pornographic bathroom fixtures and then a Roman Catholic convent; the transformation of the cult leader Consolata from a lush to a charismatic guru is more convenient than convincing. But the main problem is that there are too many characters to keep straight and too few to care about.

Michiko Kakutani's review in the *New York Times* positively murdered it—

> . . . a heavy-handed . . . contrived, formulaic book that mechanically pits men against women, old against young, the past against the present. . . .

> Nearly every one of [the] characters is a two-dimensional cliché, thin and papery and disposable. . . .

> Plot developments are also contrived. . . .

> [T]he novel's language feels closer to the hectoring, didactic voice that warped her 1992 essay "Playing in the Dark." . . .

> There are gratuitous Biblical allusions (like comparing the story of Ruby's founders to the story of the Holy Family, turned away from the inn) and even more gratuitous suggestions that the women at the convent are feminist martyrs, like the witches of Salem. . . .

> Morrison is constantly having her characters spell out the meaning of her story.

I have quoted Kakutani's review at some length because, although it's truly brutal, as you will see, in its own way it's actually closer to the truth than any of the others. All of those bad little things Kakutani accused Toni Morrison of— and more—are part of the plan of one of the most brilliantly constructed pieces of literary mischief I've ever read. *Paradise* does things that it doesn't seem possible for novels to do. (I'd love to see the look on Kakutani's face when she discovers what *Paradise* is really about.)

## *PARADISE* EXPLAINED: WHAT THE BOOK IS REALLY ABOUT

In every other part of this book, I stressed the point that what I was saying, no matter how passionately I might believe it, was my opinion—not a fact. This is NOT an opinion—it's a fact: The critics missed dozens of important "clues" in the text, and because of that, they missed the point of the book. They misunderstood the book COMPLETELY.

THAT is a fact. (I beg you not to take my word for it. Make me prove it.)

In defense of the critics, I originally misread the book in the same way they did. After my first reading of *Paradise,* I agreed with much of what they said except for the notion, which they all held, that the novel was about Paradise LOST. It had never been Paradise—how can you lose what you never had? I apologize if I'm hurting anybody's feelings, but from Day One, Ruby was a town full of 8-rock red-necks—the Moral Minority! A few specific reactions to the book on first reading: The 16-page slaughter that opens the book is so brutal that if I didn't have to read that book to write this one, I might have stopped right there. My reaction to the next chapter, the one about Mavis, wasn't as bad as the slaughter, but I felt that if it had been written by anyone other than Toni Morrison, it would have been called Blatant Racist Stereotyping. A woman dumber than the squeaky lady in *Gone with the Wind* sitting with her barefoot children in an empty house in dim-bulb love with her Cadi-fuggin-lac. Jack. Overall, I rated the book somewhere in the low middle of TM's work. And it seemed the most "racial" of her books.

Now that I understand the novel, I feel that *Paradise* is the least racial of TM's books; if Ms. Kakutani had considered the possibility that everything she bitched about TM had done intentionally, she'd have been right; I see that everything from the slaughter of the "nuns" to the "racist" Mavis cartoon were perfectly designed pieces in a book that's so damned brilliant and subversive that I can't believe it.

I promised you proof, I'll give you proof. First I'll tell you what the book IS . . . and isn't.

*Paradise* is NOT, as it appears to be on the surface, either a Feminist Novel or a Racial Novel. *Paradise* is a myth-in-progress about reality, mythology, and God. Not only is *Paradise* about myth, it IS a myth. The form of the novel is as mythological as its content. *Paradise* is NOT for one page or one minute a realistic novel. Its characters are not real because Toni Morrison didn't intend them to be real. The plot isn't realistic because TM wanted it to be over the edge—like a myth! The novel "tries out" every kind of myth, from Biblical and Greek to witch hunts and cartoons and combinations of all of the above. Mavis (a kind of a bird) whose twins didn't give her any trouble (merely died in her Cadillac while she was shopping in Higgledy Piggledy) escapes with "canary-yellow feet" (her daughter's boots) and drops by to see her mother Birdie Goodroe?

Not realistic? No shit, Sherlock. And Mavis was the most realistic character in the book! Toni Morrison wrote one book and we read another.

Now I'll give you a taste of the intentional "mistakes" and lopsided facts in the novel—verifiable with your own eyes—that every critic that I read missed. Along the way I'll do my best to interpret what those "mistakes" mean . . . but as you will see, the fact that we MIS-interpret everything is one of the hearts of the book.

### First the Proof: How About a Taste of Those "Irrefutable Facts"

The book is filled with so many contradictions, incongruities, Yogi-Berraisms, and out-of-whack facts that I'm amazed that none of the critics picked it up. I'll give you a few examples, but there are dozens of them in the novel, so you're going to have the pleasure of detecting the rest of them yourselves. It's like being on an Easter egg hunt where a perverse genius hid the eggs. And some of the "eggs" change the meaning of the book drastically. We don't have to go any further than the first paragraph to find one of those little meaning-changing gremlins. (Page numbers refer to the Knopf hardcover.)

The famous first line of the book reads, "They kill the white girl first." Two of the top reviewers offered confident, but different, opinions of who the White Girl is.

Toni Morrison said she did that on purpose; I didn't fall for it.

I fell for something more shameful: If I had to bet on WHO the White Girl is, I'd choose Mavis. Why? Because she's the one I referred to as a racist stereotype. I can either try to pretend that I meant she was a racist stereotype of a White Girl, or I can admit that while I'm over here thinking I'm so slick, TM has taken my own preconceptions about race (the ones I was sure I didn't have) and used them to help me put my foot in my mouth. That's the kind of book this is.

The second paragraph opens with the words: "They are nine, over twice the number of the women they are obliged to stampede or kill. . . ." Anyone who's read the book knows that there are FIVE women in the Convent. Nine isn't "over twice" five. I think we can safely assume (since it was on page 1) that it wasn't an oversight.

(Why did Toni Morrison do that? And why didn't the critics notice it?)

There is one thing you can be sure of: It is NOT a mistake.

On page 13, as they slaughter the Convent women, the Morgan twins who, we are told, have such magnificent memories that they remember "the details of everything that ever happened," recall the legendary first journey of their ancestors:

> On the journey from Mississippi and two Louisiana parishes to Oklahoma, the one hundred and fifty-eight freedmen were unwelcome on each grain of soil from Yazoo to Fort Smith.

Page 95: Steward Morgan, one of the Memory Twins, recalls the story differently:

> Big Papa and Big Daddy and all seventy-nine were [lost] after leaving Fairly, Oklahoma.

No reviewer I've read has noticed that there is a discrepancy in those numbers—158 versus 79. Even more suspicious, one number is exactly double the other!

(What's going on? What's Morrison up to?)

■ Steward Morgan, the twin mentioned upstairs who remembers "every detail" of everything, refers to WALKING pneumonia as "LOCKING pneumonia."

(Yo, TM, what are you up to? Is the town genius really a bozo?)

■ In books, as in life, if you want to know the truth, you have to go to someone who has her head on straight. Patricia, the lady who works on the town's genealogy, is obviously the most efficient maiden in town. If you want the facts, just bop on over to Reliable Patricia's house. She documents everything.

So why does she say that fifteen families founded Ruby . . . and then list only 14?

(I'd be the first to admit that you have to be temporarily insane to count things like that, but I was on a mission from God to figure out this novel.)

(WHY would Toni Morrison do something like that?)

(. . . and HOW did she con me into noticing it?)

What's going on here? Everybody makes mistakes? One person sees things differently than another, interprets things differently, remembers things differently, and most people lie once in awhile—sounds more like real life than a book!—and Toni Morrison isn't going to take us by the hand and tell us who's doing what. So we have to pay attention. But there are other things, down-right ridiculous things.

■ Page one, paragraph two, the second half of the sentence we mentioned above:

> They are nine, over twice the number of the women they are obliged to stampede or kill and they have the paraphernalia for either requirement: rope, a palm leaf cross, handcuffs, Mace and sunglasses, along with clean, handsome guns.

Let's see if I have this straight: These guys are going to kill some women so they bring everything they need. A palm leaf cross? Sunglasses? I don't know about you, but I never go woman-shooting without my palm leaf cross and sunglasses?

If we had not been lulled by Toni Morrison into reading her reputation instead of her words we would have noticed that there was something profoundly idiotic about men whose women-killing kit include a palm leaf cross and sunglasses.

■ On page 12, the attackers discover a gum wrapper: Doublemint. Six lines later, we learn that the leaders of the attack are twins.

What's going on? You think you're reading a strangle slaughter mangle novel (literary version, of course), and suddenly she gives you the Doublemint Twins!

Has Toni Morrison, who is damn near the most serious woman in the universe, suddenly turned into a gag writer? What could possibly be next? What else haven't we noticed that merely threatens to change the meaning of the book?

How about "Yogi-Berraisms"? (Say WHAT!) Yogi Berra is noted for making statements that may sound perfectly reasonable if they're dropped casually into a conversation (or cleverly woven into a book) when you're feeling a little brain-dead or your attention is directed elsewhere (or you let yourself get caught reading her reputation instead of her words again). But if you do notice and examine them, they turn out to be logically (or mathematically or linguistically) impossible, ridiculous, or absolutely meaningless. In the immortal words of Yogi Berra: "If they don't want to go to the ballpark, you can't keep 'em out."

I must be out of my mind, right? Toni Morrison would never do anything as dumb and outrageous as that, right? Wrong. Toni's Berraisms are every bit as ridiculous as Yogi's. But Toni's are what I would call deconstructed Yogi-Berraisms. Yogi give you the fully constructed sentence—The Stupid WHOLE—which you can separate into its Stupid PARTS. Toni give you the Stupid PARTS; if you want to know what they add up to, or mean, you simply put the Stupid PARTS together, combine them and see what Stupid WHOLE they "add up to." (Or don't add up to.) An example or two?

After reading *Paradise,* you come away absolutely certain that you know more about the citizens of Ruby, Oklahoma, their ancestors, their history, their town's history, than you've ever known about any book, ever. You can recite their history backward and forward.

Wanna bet? What you CAN do is recite an endless list of facts, *one at a time.*

What you canNOT do is put them together and make any kind of sense. Take the collapse of Haven, the first town. It was founded in 1890, survived the Depression in '32, then collapsed in '34, after the men came home from World War II. The implication is that World War II, which took place in the 1940s, caused the collapse of Haven in 1934!

And if you try to put together the facts of the legendary first journey, you end up with something like: By the time they reached Oklahoma, the Old Founders totaled 158 (page 13); they went into Fairly, but they were refused admittance, so all 79 (page 95) of them left!

Like any good Yogism, the Whole is Less than the Sum of the Parts. Those are just a few of the dozens of Yogi-Morrisonisms spread lavishly throughout the novel. They are, among other things, "clues" that tell you with a wink that if you read the book straight, you're going to miss it by a mile. None of the critics noticed any of those things, which is why I say I KNOW they blew it. There's certainly room for debate on how we should read it, but it's clear that we should NOT read it either straight or carelessly. But what's the point of all

---

### Name Games

**Steward**—one who manages other people's property or finances.

**Deacon**—(skip the noun, go straight to the verb, smile when you define it, and you'll remember it forever) adulterate (the sucker adulterated not only with Consolata, but I wouldn't be surprised if he did his sister).

**Big Papa** [Zechariah] **Morgan**—the twins' grandfather, whose real name was Coffee and who had an estranged brother named Tea.

**Big Daddy** (Rector) **Morgan**—the twins' father; a RECTOR is the clergyman in charge of the parish who owns the money collected from it.

**Grace**—the Graces were Greek goddesses of fertility who often appeared nude (as did Gigi/Grace). Grace, in Christian theology, is UNearned salvation—a gift.

**Consolata**—console, offer comfort or solace in a time of distress.

**Pallas**—Pallas Athena, Greek Goddess of Wisdom (and a species of cat!). Our girl is more cat than goddess; on two separate occasions, people say, "Here, pussy." But Pallas's main function, as you will see, is neither of the above . . .

**Divine**—(2nd definition) coming from a god.

those cartoon characters and out-of-whack facts and other winks and nods and lies of omission?

How does it all connect?

*Paradise* is a myth about the relationship between myth and truth—or, on a less lofty level, about the relationship between story telling and reality. It is a myth about how myths are formed, changed, and DE-formed. A myth is usually part of a people's oral (as opposed to written) history, so everything in it has to be extreme, larger (or smaller) than life, exaggerated: "unquestionably worthy" Good Guys battling Unspeakably Evil Bad Guys, easy to remember and cartoon clear (and even then, half of the time people are going to fugg it up). Mavis, mint green Caddy, Higgledy Piggledy, canary-yellow feet, Birdie Goodroe. And Seneca going to Wichita to see Eddie Turtle's mother and work for Norma Fox!! You see the word Doublemint and Twins jumps into your mind. A "straight" novel wouldn't name the twins Deacon and Steward and make them literal versions of their dictionary definitions—but they are. Mavis the bird, whose twins Merle and Pearl didn't give her any trouble while she was in Higgledy Piggledy, put on her yellow feet, stole the mint green Cadillac, and went to see her mommie Birdie Goodroe. Cartoons!

But knowing Toni Morrison, we have every right to suspect that there's more going on than cartoons, cartoons, car-toons, toons toons (ideally, that should be cartoony in itself while making you subconsciously aware that we may be saying a thing or two about *Jazz* in the next ten minutes).

Take for example Seneca . . .

## $S$ENECA   ≈≈≈≈≈≈≈≈≈≈≈≈≈≈≈≈≈≈≈≈≈≈≈≈≈≈≈≈≈≈

Seneca was a Roman Stoic philosopher, statesman, and author (first century A.D.). He wrote three treatises called *Consolationes*. (Consolata, arguably the heroine of *Paradise*, goes off on long speeches in Latin; Seneca wrote in Latin.)

Seneca created a sub-category of literature known as the "Senecan tragedies," a body of nine "closet dramas"—intended to be read rather than acted. (*Paradise* has nine Patriarchs, nine Founding Families, nine killers, and is constructed in nine sections named after nine women.) When Seneca's tragedies were rediscovered in the 16th century, few people in Renaissance Europe had ever seen the original Greek plays, so they thought that Seneca's were the Real Thing. Seneca's imitations—reworkings of original Greek tragedies by Euripides, Aeschylus, and Sophocles—

became the models for the revival of "Greek" tragedy during the Renaissance. According to the *Encyclopaedia Britannica*, Seneca's plays:

- "differ from the originals in . . . their obtrusive moralizing, and their bombastic rhetoric"
- "The characters are static . . . and they rant" (. . . which sounds a lot like Michiko Kakutani's bad rap on *Paradise* in the *Times*)
- "They dwell on detailed accounts of horrible deeds" (. . . a perfect description of the slaughter at the Convent)
- They "contain long reflective soliloquies"
- They are (in)famous for their "moral hairsplitting" (. . . if that doesn't fit Reverend Misner to a tee . . .)

> ### Literally Deconstructing and Reconstructing Reality
>
> At times, *Paradise* is shattering on a realistic level, even as it is sliding home a metaphor as smooth as a razor into your neck: Deek Morgan, who had fought in World War II, knew that when men were killed in war their bodies didn't stay in one piece, they flew apart, so "what they pulled off the train platform in Middleton, was a collection of parts. . . . Easter and Scout [his sons] were in integrated units. . . . If Soane [his wife] suspected what was likely—oh, man. . . . He did not want her even to imagine the single question he put to Roger [the undertaker]—first with Scout then with Easter: Are all the parts black?"

Since the Senecan tragedies were Seneca's versions of the original Greek plays, the two approaches to writing—and to life—are invariably compared. If you want to know the difference between Seneca's and the Greeks' view of man's relation to the gods, read the argument in *Paradise* between Rev. Pulliam and Rev. Misner. It's so precisely parallel that there's no doubt Toni Morrison did it intentionally. The short version goes like this.

Greek tragedy presented a world that was moral and rational; when things got tough, you could ask the gods to help you and sometimes they would—but in the end you always got what you deserved. (Even if you had to give it to yourself.)

Senecan tragedy presented a world in which only an idiot expected reason or fairness. His plays all ended with a tirade that said essentially what old fire-breathing Rev. Pulliam said: What makes you so damned arrogant that you think the gods are interested in you?

This is fun, but let's get closer to the book's center . . .

≈≈≈≈≈≈≈≈≈≈≈≈≈≈≈≈≈≈≈≈≈≈≈≈≈≈≈≈≈≈≈≈≈≈≈≈≈≈≈≈≈≈≈≈

## Who Is Telling Us This Story (and Why Are They Screwing It Up)?

When a writer like Morrison puts something as tilted as the "nine [is] over twice" five stuff on page 1, it's like an alarm. She's trying to wake us up. She's trying to tell us something. But what is she trying to tell us? Who is making that mistake and why? Are they dumb, careless, lying, or none of the above? I tried everything I could think of to figure out the Mathematically Challenged Narrator, but what finally led to a breakthrough was giving in to the feeling that *Jazz* and *Paradise* were connected. TM said that she'd originally conceived of *Beloved, Jazz,* and *Paradise* as a trilogy. What if she hadn't completely "disconnected" them? What if . . . I had it!

Two of the last things that happened in *Jazz* were Felice telling Joe Trace about the apple—a direct reference to Joe's story of Adam and Eve in the Garden of Eden (Eden is the original Paradise); and Felice telling Joe and Violet about her "unusual" friendship with Dorcas—unusual precisely because it was a friendship between a light-skinned African-American girl and a dark-skinned one. Too much like the problem the Founding Fathers faced in Fairly (alliteration—words beginning with the same letter—is another device found in songs, poems, and myths) to be a coincidence.

In a sense, *Paradise* was taking up where *Jazz* left off. The most notable thing about the way *Jazz* ended was its bizarre Narrator. It sounded like God in Her Hair Rollers over a cup of coffee—but It made mistakes; It got things wrong; It couldn't be trusted. On page 1 of *Paradise* TM is telling us

> Reviewers weren't the only ones conned by TM's novel: A few days after I made the insane but important discovery that Pat Best had said there were 15 Founding Families but listed only 14, I awoke with the realization that I'd been had: I didn't count those names because I was obsessive as I thought (there had to be a reason, that was the only one I could think of . . . he said, as he reconstructed reality). I counted those names because TM had manipulated me into it.
>
> This is how she did it: of all the Founding Families, three names stood out—DuPres and Beauchamp (French) and Blackhorse (Native American). To me, Blackhorse not only seemed the most unusual, the Blackhorse family had been mentioned several times in the preceding pages. Guess which name was missing from the 15 Founding Families? The absence of that one name overpowered the presence of the other 14.

that this novel too has a narrator that makes mistakes, that gets things wrong, that can't be trusted.

Next Question: The Narrator who opens the book and gets things wrong—who is it? Is it Toni Morrison? Or God? Technically it was from the "collective viewpoint" of the nine attackers—which was both ridiculous and impossible, unless all nine people think one thought—so I decided that I was missing the point. No matter who the narrator was, it was unreliable; it couldn't be trusted. Was TM implying that even God was an Unreliable Narrator? (Let's save that question for later.) Morrison isn't saying THIS narrator is unreliable. She seems to be saying that ALL narrators are unreliable. (Including herself.)

> **Double Your Pleasure . . .**
>
> TM uses the Doubling or Twinning technique to the point of ridiculousness. Dozens of comparings, contrastings, pairings, and twins, baby—you never saw so many twins!—literal twins, figurative twins, twin situations, twin histories—it's like Noah's Ark: there's two of everything! Deek & Steward are twins; Mavis's dead babies are twins; Mavis had two brothers killed in Vietnam; Deek & Sloane had two sons killed in Vietnam; two attempts at Paradise; two Ovens; two town histories; Big Papa & Big Daddy; Old Fathers & New Fathers; Ruby juxtaposed to the Convent; the original whory version of the Convent contrasted with the nun's version; two opposing preachers, two versions of God; a Cross with Jesus & a Cross without—I could go on, but the question is: What is the Doubling getting at? What's TM trying to tell us?

She's also saying that whatever information we're given we have to interpret. In the opening scene of the novel, although we can't prove it until later, we know that those gun-totin' God-on-their-side maniacs are misinterpreting everything they see: they're absolutely certain that Seneca's written-in-lipstick letter is a "satanic message" "written in blood" and they expect to find even more "evidence."

TM is also saying what psychologists and police have said for years: all witnesses are unreliable. In the book's last chapter, everyone, including the people who'd been at the Convent and seen the slaughter with their own eyes, had a different version of what had happened. Even Lone DuPres, who by that time stood as the person most deserving of respect, had remembered, interpreted, and processed the slaughter so that it added up to something coherent. And by shifting things around, she even made it cohere with the rest of her life. (Oh, damn, if I had followed my instincts about those birds that appeared at K.D. and Arnette's wedding, I would have known . . . bip bip bip.)

As TM put it when she described the people in *Beloved,* we "deconstruct reality" and "reconstruct" it until it "fits," no matter what we have to add, subtract, change, or ignore. That is the way we construct our myths, it is the way we construct our pasts, and it is the way we construct everyday "reality." What Toni Morrison does next is ingenious, beautifully underhanded, and completely impossible. Morrison has "rigged" *Paradise* so that the critics not only complete her novel, they actually prove its thesis—even if they think they're denying it! Impossible, right? Check it out.

The opening of *Paradise,* no matter how much you hate the dispassionate violence, is so arresting that virtually every reviewer quotes the first two paragraphs. Although good critics are surely some of the smartest people on the planet, it isn't fair to expect even them to connect a couple facts separated by two or three hundred pages. But over half of the reviewers, after quoting the opening of Morrison's novel—inside the review that they themselves wrote—go on to say that the shooters killed five women. "They are nine, over twice the number of the women they are obliged to . . . kill" . . . and they killed FIVE women? On the dumbest day of their lives, none of those brainy men and women would think than nine was over two-times-five—yet no reviewer that I read mentioned it; they had so thoroughly "reconstructed" reality that they put the incompatible facts into the reviews they wrote without even noticing it. Thus the reviewers complete Morrison's novel by proving her thesis right before our eyes: we do whatever we must to make sense of the world, even if it takes turning so dumb in one little square inch of our lives that it never occurs to us that nine isn't more than "twice" five.

### The Presence of Something Absent

There were two motifs in *Paradise* that recurred too often not to be important: one was an idea phrased in different ways, stressing "the presence" of something "absent"; the other was the technique of Twinning or Doubling (see chapters on *The Bluest Eye* and *Sula* if your memory died). I used both concepts to break through to the idea that *Paradise* started where *Jazz* ended—but they led me to some other interesting places that I haven't yet mentioned . . .

When I let "the presence of something absent" roll around in my hat with the ideas of Twinning, Doubling, Contrasting, Comparing, and everything in Twos, what I settled on as the guiding image or metaphor is the Other Side of the Coin, the Mirror Image, the Opposite, confusing Figure and Ground. Whatever I see, isn't what it's about. (Steward's wife Dovey defined her husband by what he'd lost, not by what he'd gained.) Whatever you specify, I should turn the word over like a coin and look at the other side. There's nothing outlandish about that. If a writer points out the Asians and blacks and Latinos, it's a pretty sure bet that he is None of the Above. You are at the center of the world you create . . . and the only way I can find you is to look in the spaces between the things you specify. (A few pages back, I said I suspected that Mavis was The White Girl precisely because I thought she wasn't; I went back to her chapter to see if there was anything that would verify my "hunch." Sure enough, when Mavis sees Soane, her reaction is: "The black woman opened her arms." Other confirming clues follow.) So if Toni Morrison titles the novel *Paradise*, that's exactly what it isn't about. Does that mean it's about Hell? There's no evidence to support that; I think the title is simply ironic. High sarcasm, baby.

We know that TM started out with the intention of making *Beloved, Jazz,* and *Paradise* a trilogy and eventually changed her mind. The only connection she still acknowledges between the books is that each of them is about a certain kind of love taken to excess. *Beloved* is about excessive love of one's children, *Jazz* is about romantic love taken to excess, and *Paradise* is about love of God taken to excess. If I "translate" those three statements into the way most of us think of them, but turn them into *operations*—into the *actions* that speak louder than words—we get:

I love my daughter so much that under certain circumstances I would kill her.
I love that woman so much that under certain circumstances I would kill her.

But when it comes to God, most of us take the notion of excessive love of God to mean, approximately, I love my God so much that under certain circumstances I would kill people who don't believe in Him. There are a couple things wrong with that: it's completely out of symmetry with the other two, and it seems a little too obvious or common for the fiercely original Morrison. To make her "love of God" statement stand in symmetry with the others, you'd have to perform a couple of operations on it. You'd have to say: I love God so much that under certain circumstances I would kill *Him*.

Not kill other people *for* Him—kill Him. I am not exactly sure what that means, but it feels scary enough to satisfy even Toni Morrison. But it's still not quite in symmetry with the first two premises, is it? Maybe we miss the heart and soul of *Paradise* unless we make Toni Morrison's three Love/Kill statements perfectly symmetrical:

> I love my daughter so much that under certain circumstances I would kill *her.*
> I love that woman so much that under certain circumstances I would kill *her.*
> I love God so much that under certain circumstances I would kill *Her.*

I thought I was smiling when I said that, but to my utter astonishment, I think I'm serious. The good citizens of Ruby didn't kill any "hims," they killed five "hers." What if *Paradise* was not about the town of Ruby or Haven or the Founding Fatheads?

What if it was about the Convent?

What if *Paradise* is not the story of the men's mythology at all?

It's the Women's. (I scared myself with that one. I'd better shut up before the Goddess strikes me with lightning.)

In the process of trying to figure out *Jazz,* I'd gone from the epigraph in front of the novel to John Leonard's epic review of *Jazz* (*Nation,* 1992) to see what that incomprehensible epigraph could possibly mean. What Leonard said didn't help me with *Jazz,* but, honey, it sure does go straight to the heart of *Paradise:*

> Picking up on the epigraph to *Jazz*—from "Thunder, Perfect Mind" in The Nag Hammadi—and knowing that Morrison now spends part of every week . . . with Elaine Pagels, who wrote the book on The Gnostic Gospels, I said, "Aha!" "Thunder, Perfect Mind" is the revelation of a feminine power: "I am the whore, and the holy one. I am the wife and the virgin. I am [the mother] and the daughter. . . ."

Not only did it verify the fact that TM had done some serious thinking about female gods, but it reminds us that female gods were often goddesses of fertility—sexy gods—so it rhymed perfectly with the fact the Convent started out as a porno playground.

What about *Paradise*'s epigraph? A novel's epigraph is the first place you look to get a handle on the book's meaning, but *Paradise*'s epigraph is not only vague, it is unattributed—TM didn't say where she'd taken it from; she could have written it herself. I had a hunch: I picked up a copy of Elaine Pagels's *The Gnostic Gospels* along with the full Nag Hammadi text. As I suspected, the epigraph in *Paradise* was taken from "The Thunder, Perfect Mind"—"the revelation of a feminine power."

BAM! No question about it: I was zeroing in on the center of the novel.

### "The Thunder . . ." and Other Perfect Minds

The lines quoted by John Leonard ("I am the whore, and the holy one. . . .") are probably the high point of the seven-page "Thunder, Perfect Mind," but the quality of the poetry is inconsequential in light of what the piece is— namely, a "divine revelation" by a Christian female god. Not a saint—a god. She draws parallels between herself and the gods of Greece and Egypt. By what she says, you can tell she's not the only god or the top god, but if there's a hierarchy, she's probably Number Two. Incredible!—a polytheistic Christianity with a female god (or gods) on the Board of Directors! "Thunder, Perfect Mind" wasn't the only Female god envisioned by the agile-minded Gnostics.

The Gnostics were among the earliest Christians, but we didn't know much about them because the orthodox Christians burned the Gnostic writings. In 1945 an Egyptian "peasant" (does anyone ever call himself a peasant?) found dozens of Gnostic manuscripts in the village of Nag Hammadi. The Gnostic writings discovered there—gospels; revelations; alternative views of God, gods, Jesus, women (secular and divine), creation—give us an idea of what the Gnostics believed—and of what Christianity almost became.

### Gnostic Female Divinities

Several of the Gnostic gospels describe a Female god who is Number One, with a Male god who assists her (She thinks it, He builds it). The Female god is usually Silent and Invisible—she can't be seen; she must be intuited (just like in Morrison's *Paradise*). Sometimes Female and Male are separate gods, sometimes they're different aspects of a single god. Sometimes there is only One god, but It is a Trinity comprised of the Father, the Son, and the Mother.

> What's with this "us" crap? Toni Morrison asks those questions for "her" people— since I am not quite black (merely an Arab) she isn't speaking to me, right? I don't know about you, but she speaks to me. The "specificity of detail" with which she sings of "her" people makes her work more applicable to non-blacks, not less.

The point: Even though modern Christianity (and the other Big Daddy monotheisms) is one of the only religions in history that does NOT have a Female god, Monotheistic Maleness is NOT necessarily a "commandment" of Christianity, as evidenced by the fact that many of the Gnostics (who considered *themselves* the orthodox Christians and the *other guys* the heretics) assumed the existence of Female gods in one form or another. Not only that, as Elaine Pagels points out in her book, the "Church's" choices were more political than theological: Men who want to control women find it easier to justify if God is a Guy—and men who want to control everybody favor monotheism because they can "theologically" justify ruling their turf with an Iron Fist.

# *B*LACK ATHENA ≈≈≈≈≈≈≈≈≈≈≈≈≈≈≈≈≈≈≈≈≈≈≈≈≈≈≈

> Who controls the past
> controls the future;
> who controls the present
> controls the past.
> —George Orwell, *1984*

Why did Toni Morrison name the young pregnant girl Pallas, and then give her nothing in common with Pallas Athena, the Greek goddess she's named for? Because (speculation, not fact) TM wants us to leap over the goddess to *Black Athena*, the semi-famous books by Martin Bernal. Most people assume from the title that Bernal's books set out to prove that some of the Greek gods were black. That's one implication of *Black Athena*, but Bernal's aim is broader than a debate over the complexion of the gods. Bernal means to prove that the entire civilization of Classical

Greece that we consider the foundation of Western culture is neither Greek nor Western, it's African and Middle Eastern. Bernal supports his argument by quoting Greek historians from the Classical period who say in no uncertain terms that Greek culture in its entirety was the result of colonization by Egyptians and Phoenicians. In Bernal's words:

> Black Athena is focused on Greek cultural borrowings from Egypt and the Levant in the thousand years from 2100 to 1100 bc.

Why, you ask, don't we know that? Because European historians falsified Greek history. Why did Europeans falsify history? They were enslaving millions of Africans. Civilized people would never enslave human beings, so Europeans had to make Africans appear sub-human. Egypt was in Africa; if they admitted that Egyptians were the source of Greek culture, they'd be admitting that Africans were not only human, but their own "cultural forefathers." It was cheaper and less embarrassing to rewrite history than to give those slaves their freedom and the intellectual credit they

---

### The EMPOWERED 8-ROCK INTERPRETATION

The New Founders realized they couldn't live strong lives while maintaining the mythology of their ancestors, so they built a new one and lived less unhappily ever after.

This interpretation allows you to believe (without demanding it) that the slaughter at the Convent never took place. Even symbolically, it was not about murder, it was about the process of inventing the myths you need to live your life in the way you'd like; the great advantage of myths is that you can benefit from them without doing them; so the men didn't literally kill any women (one reason you call it a myth is because it never happened); and you don't have to fuss over whether the women escaped alive or were saved in some magical way; the important thing was that the myth "wanted" to make its point without leaving a pile of unsightly female corpses around. With the proper myth, you can have your cake and eat it too.

This can't be the primary interpretation of the novel because it leaves out too many other important things. Like Female Divinity . . .

---

deserved! (The nerve of those bastards, inventing OUR culture!) Bernal calls the new Whitebread history the Aryan Model and fairly shocks us with this:

Most people are surprised to learn that the Aryan Model, which most of us have been brought up to believe, developed only during . . . the 19th century.

Bernal contends that virtually the whole of Greek civilization—Greek language, philosophy, science, politics, even the famous "city-state"—was borrowed or derived from Egypt and Phoenicia. He traces the Greek gods back to their Egyptian and Phoenician ancestors: "Athena was the Egyptian Neit and the Semitic Anat [etc.]." To what "race" did the Egyptians belong? For 7,000 years Egypt has contained African, Southwest Asian, and Mediterranean "types"; the further south you go, the higher the ratio of black Africans. And the Egyptian civilization?—"fundamentally African." The African influence was stronger in the Old and Middle Kingdoms and "many of the most powerful pharaohs [were] black." No surprises there, just common sense. Like the contention that many of the "Greek" gods were black.

≈≈≈≈≈≈≈≈≈≈≈≈≈≈≈≈≈≈≈≈≈≈≈≈≈≈≈≈≈≈≈≈≈≈≈≈≈≈≈≈≈≈≈

> Female divinities?
> Myths-in-progress?
> Unreliable Narrators?
> Intentional "mistakes"?
> Contradictions?
> Gags?
> Yogi-Berraisms?
> Deconstructing?
> Reconstructing?
> Misinterpreting?
> Senecan Tragedies?
> Black Athenas?
> 8-rocks?
> . . . and all the other things?

## What in the Hell Does It All Mean?

We have all the pieces, but we're missing something basic, something that will give us the key to how the pieces come together to make the Novel whole—more than merely the sum of its parts. It is the difference between a pile of body parts and a living, breathing human being.

So far, whenever I've been stuck for an answer, the mind-set that's helped unlock me is assuming that TM's last three novels—the "disconnected" Trilogy—are connected in some way that will help me see the overall aim of *Paradise*.

## The CONVENT Women's Interpretation

The Convent women were innocent victims—but were they goddesses? I seriously doubt that Toni M intended that (except for Consolata, who we'll get to in a minute). But were they martyrs? The Christian martyrs who have gone down in history aren't famous because they were gods; their only claim to fame is that they were eaten by lions. So, yes, the women qualify as martyrs.

There is another dimension to the slaughter of the women that I'll describe in a bit more detail in the Biblical Interpretations. For now, note that the 8-Rockers' slaughter of the Convent women had a conspicuously self-righteous Biblical tone, not unlike the Old Testament Hebrew prophets, who don't get nearly enough credit for being intolerant religious fanatics. On more than one occasion, inspired by God's word (just like the 8-Rockers), the old Hebrews slaughtered "pagan" temples full of "evil priestesses."

Is Consolata a god/goddess? To the extent that the novel is to be taken literally, yes, absolutely. She is not only resurrected, she ends the novel in the position of Jesus in the Pietà (see "Piedade" next door).

The mythologist Joseph Campbell had some interesting things to say about the evolution of Jesus. Campbell said that most cultures had gods who were gentle and loving and, if need be, willing to sacrifice themselves. Campbell said that the only original thing about Jesus was that He was a man. Christianity had taken a typical Female God and turned Her into a Man. Did Toni Morrison turn Him back into a woman?

This interpretation is better . . . but it still leaves a lot out. *Paradise* is about a lot more than Female gods . . .

Are they connected in any way other than the ways we've mentioned? I'd bet Norman Mailer's left testicle on it; not only are they connected, but the connection plugs into one of the central projects of Toni Morrison's life. In her own famous words—

"Our past was appropriated. I am one of the people who has to reappropriate it."

One of the ways that Toni Morrison approaches the huge task of reappropriating the past is by exploring in fiction different ways of dealing with it. How do we deal with an intensely traumatic past? How do we rid ourselves of the scars and deformities the past has imposed on us so we can go about the business of living focused and powerful lives?

Toni Morrison's non-Trilogy deals with the past in the same way it dealt with excessive love. Just as the three books are about three different kinds of

---

### The MODELED-ON-THE-BIBLE Interpretation

Every reviewer mentioned it—some as a symbol of the Old Founders' "Exodus," others as "gratuitous Biblical allusions." On my good days, I realize that if you resist an insight, it often tries to sneak into consciousness disguised as humor—but when I said several pages back, "This book has more names than the Bible," it never occurred to me that TM might be trying to tell us that it was (sort of) the Bible. It seemed too obvious to take seriously—Old Founders, New Founders; Old Testament, New Testament. The Old Founders had an Exodus; obviously, so did the Old Testament guys. Zechariah was a leader who helped restore Israel after they left Babylon. Big Papa was named Zechariah. After the Disallowing, the 8-Rocks considered themselves Chosen People (I don't even have to finish that one, do I?)

There's no reason to believe that the whole novel is modeled on the Bible, but there is justification for noting that the 8-Rocks (both Old and New) modeled their own mythology on the Bible. With apologies to those of you who can't abide the thought of a humorous Bible, I feel obliged to point out that at times *Paradise* seems like a slapstick version of the Good Book. The 8-Rockers have modeled their myth on the Bible ridiculously, absurdly. (Dear Ms. Kakutani, when the New Founders put on a Christmas play with SEVEN Holy Families, didn't it occur to you that it was meant to be funny and doesn't Pat Best's obsessive genealogy remind you of one of those "begat" sections of the Bible—A begat B, B begat C, etc?)

---

love-taken-to-excess, they're also about three different ways of dealing-with-the-past:

> *Beloved* is about trying to FORGET (or repress) the past.
> *Jazz* is about trying to IGNORE (or "skip over") the past.
> *Paradise* is about RE-INVENTING (or re-writing) the past.

If we combine a couple of the things we know, phrase it a few different ways, we get . . .

> *Paradise* is a Myth about people who are BADLY in NEED of re-inventing the Past?
> *Paradise* is a Myth about people who are BADLY in NEED of a New Myth?
> *Paradise* is a story about somebody whose Myth BADLY needs fixin'?

**Key Question:** WHO is that somebody whose Myth BADLY needs fixin'?

There are a few different possibilities. Let's check them out. The interpretation that offers itself on the surface of the novel is the one from Reverend Misner. Let's call it The Empowered 8-Rock Interpretation.

The Empowered 8-Rock Interpretation raises several questions and a few problems. But first, Two Possibilities that apply to any of the interpretations: (1) The possibility exists that Haven and the Disallowing and the Old Founders may have been totally fabricated—they may never have happened; or (2) They may have happened twice: the New Founders may have repeated exactly what the Old Founders had done. (Just before the slaughter, Soane and Dovey try to convince themselves that their men won't kill the Convent women. Soane says, "They're different is all." Dovey replies, "I know, but that's been enough before.") That "before" is ominous.

Question: When Reverend Misner says that the townspeople simply recite the heroics of their ancestors but say nothing about themselves, that "They don't want children, they want duplicates," is he speaking "for" the novel? Per-

---

### The Critical-of-the-Bible Interpretation

Feeling like the chump who gets shot for delivering the message (or is it like the guy who flunked his Rorsach test and said, What do you mean *I* have a filthy mind—*you're* the one who drew the dirty pictures!), I do believe that Ms. Toni is being severely critical of the Bible in this novel. No matter how you cut it, *Paradise* is a critique of the Judaeo-Christian patriarchal view of the world expressed in the Bible, especially (but not only) the Old Testament. The parallel between the Biblical Hebrews and 8-Rocks is indisputable, severely critical, and funny. Both the Hebrews and the 8-Rocks claimed to be Chosen People; both purported to make a Covenant with God; both excluded from "Paradise" everyone but themselves; and neither could bear the presence of free women.

Around 800 B.C., Jehu, a soldier famous for his brutality, was chosen by the prophet Elisha for a special mission. Jehu and his men tracked down the Phoenician woman Jezebel, called her a whore, accused her of being a witch, and killed her. Then they gathered worshippers of the Phoenician god Baal inside a temple and slaughtered them. (I wouldn't be surprised if Toni Morrison used that slaughter as a "model" for the killing of the convent women in *Paradise*.)

One thing is obvious. In slaughtering the Convent women, the good citizens of Ruby, Oklahoma, were not creating a new myth.

They were replaying an ancient one.

haps even for TM her self? (Lord, I hope not.) My main complaint with this interpretation is that no matter how you pretty it up or mythologize it, those guys slaughtered five women—and they did it in what French philosopher Jean Paul Sartre would call "bad faith" (they bullshitted themselves every step of the way). If we accept this interpretation, we reward them for their murder and self-deception.

We have already accepted the fact that *Paradise* is in some way about a Female God or gods. Does that make the Convent Women the central figures in a new mythology? If so, what are their roles? Are they also the people "whose Myth BADLY needs fixin'," or merely the central figures in the new Myth that the sad sack citizens of Ruby, Oklahoma, so dearly need?

Louis Menand, writing in the *New Yorker,* cracked, "but did it have to have four resurrections?" (Wisecrack often reveal hidden truth, Grasshopper.) I laughed at first, and in The Empowered 8-Rock Interpretation, I sidestepped the question of whether the Convent women were killed, not killed, killed but "their spirits" lived on, or they actually died and came back to life—resurrected!—by saying it didn't matter because it was a myth and all the myth needed was not to have innocent corpses muddying up the ending.

I was wrong: It mattered. And it wasn't four resurrections, it was five—and a Cadillac! (The "emerald eyed" young woman with her head on Piedade's lap is Consolata.) Speaking of Piedade—

### Piedade

Piedade, the mystery creature who ends the novel, who or what is it? Piedade is Pietà, Mother Mary with dead Jesus on her lap (picture Michelangelo's statue). Last page of *Paradise:* "Next to her is a younger woman whose head rests on the singing woman's lap." The head-on-the-lap position is considered the "realistic" version of the Pietà *(Encyclopaedia Britannica).* The older woman (the Mother Mary figure) is "black as firewood"; the "younger woman" (the Jesus figure?) has emerald eyes (Consolata). Mother, Daughter, Holy Ghostess?

Let's consider one other possibility—maybe our search shouldn't be on the somebody whose Myth needs fixin', but on the Myth itself? The one myth that *Paradise* keeps disappearing into the shadow of is the Bible.

The question is, is *Paradise* modeled on the Bible . . . or critical of it?

I had asked awhile back whether Reverend Misner was the book's spokesman? In some ways he seems to be: parts of his rap could have been taken out of Pagels's *The Gnostic Gospels* almost verbatim; other parts are almost word-for-word textbook descriptions of the difference between the Greek world view and Seneca's world view. But as close as he is in words, his spirit seems opposite the spirit of the novel. Misner badmouths the townspeople for trying to live in the 20th century with 19th-century myths without noticing that the mythology he has devoted his entire life to is two thousand years old, has a gaping hole in it where a Female god belongs, and (some would say) has nothing whatsoever to do with the world we live in now.

I have no respect for people who neglect to mention things that contradict their tidy theories; I not only admit that this critical-of-the-Bible view is contrary to everything I know about TM's attitude toward Christianity, I'll put her on the phone so she can contradict me herself. In the interview with Charles Ruas, Toni Morrison explained with striking eloquence why Christianity has been so important to black people:

> It was the love things that were psychically very important. Nobody could have endured that life in constant rage. They would have all gone mad. . . . You do something that destroys yourself, or else you give up. But with the love thing . . . they could sublimate the other things [and] transcend them.

There were some things that they simply didn't do:

> They didn't commit suicide, they didn't stone people . . . they were better than that. What made them better was this very pure, very aristocratic love that made them the most civilized people in the world. That was their dignity, how they transcended.

Am I certain that Morrison's *Paradise* is critical of Christianity? No, I'm not—but it seems to be what the novel is saying—and repeating with added vinegar and considerable sarcasm by the All-Knowing But Unreliable Narrator of the Consolata chapter. A person referred to as the "benefactress" has bought the mansion and turned it into a convent "to bring God and language to natives who were assumed to have neither; to alter their diets, their clothes, their

minds; to help them despise everything that had once made their lives worth-
while and to offer them instead the privilege of knowing the one and only God
and a chance, thereby, for redemption."

The previous interpretation was Modeled on the Bible; this one is Critical of it. Toni Morrison seems to have noticed with a vengeance that the Bible
is the . . . the *Bible* of Eurocentric White Male Mythology. Once again, given
her love of Christianity in the past, it's surprising to see her being so critical of
it. On the other hand, given her brainy honesty and her zero tolerance for
White Male Eurocentric anything, it's surprising that it took her so long to notice it.

Let's have a go at the Big Question.

## Is God the Ultimate Unreliable Narrator?

TM seems to imply that in the novel. After Consolata brings a dead person
back to life, she begins praying because she thinks she's offended God. Lone
DuPres, her "adviser," tells her to stop being such a wuss and do what God
wants her to do. Consolata answers, "I think He wants me to ignore *you*" (my
emphasis).

And the endless arguments between the preachers (and between Reverend
Misner and himself)? I think that Toni Morrison is saying that even if there IS
only One God, He's such an Unreliable Narrator that we don't know if He's a
Baptist, Methodist, Pentecostal, Catholic, Native American, former Chicago
Bulls basketball player, Brazilian voodooist, Jew, Muslim, Buddhist, Feminist,
or a Trickster God who wants to drive us all crazy . . .

Or you can put it like the Danish philosopher Kierkegaard did: No mat-
ter what God tells you, YOU have to decide if the Voice you hear is The Real
God or A False God or the Devil or One God among Many or the Masculine
Half of a Dual-Gender God or some Supersmoke or a Hallucination or You
Telling Yourself What You'd Like to Hear . . . or a Secret Government Plot to
Take over Your Mind.

Whether God is an Unreliable Narrator or we're Unreliable Interpreters, it
amounts to the same thing: God doesn't make your choices—you do.

## WHERE DOES THE NOVEL END (AND LIFE BEGIN)?

All of the above interpretations tell us something about the novel—but none of them answers the last Basic Question we need to know the Heart of the Novel:

Whose myths are dysfunctional enough to die from?
Who is so badly in need of a New Mythology?
Who is the novel speaking to?
WHO?

Finally . . . I had it.

(It was so obvious that you probably beat me to it.) *Paradise* wasn't about the people in the book, it was about us.

It's our myths that need fixin'.

It's our myths that don't match Reality.

It's our Bible that pretends that God, not man, denies equal status to women; and it's our perversion of God's Voice that divides the world into Us and Them, then excludes everyone but Us from Paradise.

It's our historians who have sanitized history-book slavery until it seemed like just another "job" that people of African descent had a natural talent for.

It's our selectively blind media and self-mythologizing education system that allow us to be so simpleminded in one little square inch of our lives at a time that we can't spot the simplest contradictions: a democratic, equal-opportunity country in which women and people of color get paid one-third less than white males; the richest country in the world where one out of every four children is born into poverty; a welfare system that does its best to ignore working people who've lost their jobs but bails out billionaire savings and loan f—kups; a country that "spreads democracy" by suppressing popular movements and backing dictators.

*Paradise* is a wake-up call to a country buried in its own self-deluding excrement. We are ignoring each other to death with our own shitty myths.

It's exactly what Guitar said:

> when you release all the shit, then you can FLY.
> —"Air" Morrison, *Song of Solomon*

If you want to know exactly what *Paradise* means, I honestly believe that Toni Morrison is playing or being (or IS) the Trickster God(dess) so thoroughly that she has done what a Trickster should do: come to "inconclusive conclusions." *Paradise* is about "reading" carefully and skeptically. Reading books, life, God, each other's humanity, you name it. It's about refusing to go blind in any square inch of your life. It's about letting every half-of-something find its opposite.

> *Paradise* is one big de-constructed Yogi-Berraism.
> *Paradise* is a Trickster Bible.
> *Paradise* is a myth about some folks whose myth is busted and don't even know it until some mythical goddess appears and writes a mythical book about some folks whose myth is busted and don't even know it until some mythical goddess appears and writes a mythical book about some folks whose myth is busted . . .

*Paradise* is one of the most original novels ever written.

# AFTERTHOUGHTS

## LIKE BERGMAN AND FELLINI

My initial reaction to Toni Morrison's novels was that they didn't seem like novels at all, they seemed like movies. Not just any old movies, but like the "foreign" films of people like Bergman and Fellini and Antonioni and Godard and all those wonderful madmen who made movies—"films"—that seemed like they held the Secret of Life if only you could figure the damned things out. Good? Bad? Like? Dislike? Those concepts were wimpy, irrelevant, lifeless . . . You label one Good, label the other Bad, and walk away without caring if you ever see them again.

When we watched those mov—films—there was only question that mattered: How intensely did it engage me, provoke me, involve me? If you discussed it politely for an hour and went home, it was a Flop. If it kept you and your friends awake all night arguing like maniacs—THAT was Ecstacy.

My opinion of Morrison's novels varies radically from page to page, but they always, always engage me, provoke me, involve me. If there was anything I wanted while I was reading Toni Morrison's novels, it was the presence of other people to "rassle" with. I didn't want people to discuss Morrison's books with. I wanted people who were so passionate and intense about her books that they would stay awake all night and argue with me . . . because they felt as I felt, that even if Toni Morrison's novels pissed you off profoundly, there was something about them that was as important as life and death.

I honestly think that's the best way to read Toni Morrison's novels. Share them with friends, then go to war over them.

*Thank you, Toni Morrison*

# BIBLIOGRAPHY &
# SUGGESTED READING

■ Reprinted in *Toni Morrison: Critical Perspectives Past and Present*, edited by Henry Louis Gates, Jr., and K. A. Appiah. New York: Amistad, 1993.

● Reprinted in *Conversations with Toni Morrison*, edited by Danielle Taylor-Guthrie. Jackson: University Press of Mississippi, 1994.

◆ Reprinted in *Contemporary Black American Fiction Writers*, edited by Harold Bloom. New York: Chelsea House, 1995.

Allen, Brooke. Review of *Paradise. New York Times Book Review*, January 11, 1998.

Anderson, S. E. *The Black Holocaust for Beginners*. New York: Writers & Readers, 1995.

Angelo, Bonnie. "The Pain of Being Black: An Interview with Toni Morrison." *Time*, May 22, 1989. ●

Atwood, Margaret. Review of *Beloved. New York Times Book Review*, September 13, 1987. ■

Awkward, Michael. " 'The Evil of Fulfillment': Scapegoating and Narration in *The Bluest Eye.*" *Inspiriting Influences, Tradition, Revision, and Afro-American Women's Novels*. New York: Columbia University Press, 1989. ■

Bakerman, Jane. "The Seams Can't Show: An Interview with Toni Morrison." *Black American Literature Forum* 12.2, Summer 1978. ●

Bawer, Bruce. Review of *Playing in the Dark: Whiteness and the Literary Imagination*. *New Criterion*, Volume 10, September 1991 to June 1992.

Bernal, Martin. *Black Athena: The Afroasiatic Roots of Classical Civilization. Volume 1: The Fabrication of Ancient Greece 1785–1985.* New Brunswick: Rutgers University Press, 1987.

Bernal, Martin. *Black Athena: The Afroasiatic Roots of Classical Civilization. Volume 2: The Archaeological and Documentary Evidence.* New Brunswick: Rutgers University Press, 1991.

Blackburn, Sarah. Review of *Sula*. *New York Times Book Review*, December 30, 1973. ■

Blake, Susan L. "Folklore and Community in *Song of Solomon*." MELUS 7, No. 3, Fall 1980. ◆

Bloom, Harold. "Introduction" to *Contemporary Black American Fiction Writers*, edited by Harold Bloom. New York: Chelsea House, 1995.

Bryant, Jerry H. Review of *Sula*. *Nation*, July 6, 1974. ■◆

Caldwell, Gail. Review of *Beloved*. *Boston Globe*, October 6, 1987. ●

Century, Douglas. *Toni Morrison* (*Black Americans of Achievement* series). New York: Chelsea House, 1994.

Christian, Barbara. "The Contemporary Fables of Toni Morrison." *Black Women Novelists.* Currently out of print. (There must be a publisher out there with the brains and sensitivity to resurrect Christian's fine book.) ■

Clemmons, Walter. Review of *Beloved*. *Newsweek*, September 25, 1987. ◆

Crouch, Stanley. "Aunt Medea." *The New Republic*, October 19, 1987.

Dowling, Colette. "Interview with Morrison." *New York Times Magazine*, May 20, 1979. ●

Encyclopaedia Britannica. 1986. See entries under "Seneca" and "Senecan tragedies."

Frankel, Haskel.   Review of *The Bluest Eye. New York Times Book Review,* November 1, 1970. ■

Furman, Jan.   *Toni Morrison's Fiction* (*Understanding Contemporary American Literature* series). Columbia: University of South Carolina Press, 1996.

Gant, Liz.   Review of *The Bluest Eye. Black World,* Volume 20, May 1971.

Gates, David.   Review of *Paradise. Newsweek,* January 12, 1998.

Gates, Henry Louis, Jr.   Review of *Jazz. Toni Morrison: Critical Perspectives Past & Present,* edited by Henry Louis Gates, Jr., and K. A. Appiah. New York: Amistad, 1993.

Gray, Paul.   Review of *Beloved. Time,* September 21, 1987.

Harris, Middleton.   *The Black Book.* An anthology compiled by Middleton Harris, with the assistance of Morris Levitt, Roger Furman, Ernest Smith. Edited by Toni Morrison. New York: Random House, 1974.

Hulbert, Ann.   Review of *Playing in the Dark: Whiteness and the Literary Imagination. New Republic,* May 18, 1992.

Irving, John.   Review of *Tar Baby. New York Times Book Review,* March 29, 1981. ■

Kakutani, Michiko.   Review of *Paradise. New York Times,* January 6, 1998.

Koenen, Anna.   "The One Out of Sequence." *History and Tradition in Afro-American Culture,* edited by Gunther Lenz. Frankfurt: Campus, 1984. (The 1980 interview with Toni Morrison was published in 1984.) ●

Lardner, Susan.   Review of *Song of Solomon. New Yorker,* November 7, 1977. ■

LeClair, Thomas.   " 'The Language Must Not Sweat': A Conversation with Toni Morrison." *New Republic,* March 21, 1981. ■●

Leonard, John.   Review of *The Bluest Eye. New York Times,* November 13, 1970.

Leonard, John.   "Her Soul's High Song." Review of *Jazz. Nation,* May 25, 1992. (Leonard's review includes a long, rhapsodic recap of Toni Morrison's career.) ■

Leonard, John.   An article on Morrison receiving the Nobel Prize. *Nation,* January 17, 1994.

Mbalia, Dorthea Drummond.   *Toni Morrison's Developing Class Consciousness.* Selinsgrove, PA: Susquehanna University Press, 1991. ◆

McKay, Nellie.   "An Interview with Toni Morrison." *Contemporary Literature* 24, Winter 1983. ■●

Menand, Louis.   Review of *Paradise. New Yorker,* January 12, 1998.

Millar, Neil.   Review of *Song of Solomon. Atlantic,* October 1977.

Morrison, Toni.   *The Bluest Eye.* New York: Holt, Rinehart and Winston, 1970.

Morrison, Toni.   *Sula.* New York: Alfred A. Knopf, 1973.

Morrison, Toni.   *Song of Solomon.* New York: Alfred A. Knopf, 1977.

Morrison, Toni.   *Beloved.* New York: Alfred A. Knopf, 1987.

Morrison, Toni.   *Tar Baby.* New York: Alfred A. Knopf, 1981.

Morrison, Toni.   *Jazz.* New York: Alfred A. Knopf, 1992.

Morrison, Toni.   *Paradise.* New York: Alfred A. Knopf, 1997.

Non-fiction referred to in the book, kept separate for clarity's sake—

Morrison, Toni.   "Rediscovering Black History." *New York Times Magazine,* August 11, 1974.

Morrison, Toni.   *Playing in the Dark: Whiteness and the Literary Imagination.* Cambridge: Harvard University Press, 1992.

Morrison, Toni.   *Race[ing] Justice, [En]gender[ing] Power: Essays on Anita Hill, Clarence Thomas, and the Construction of Social Reality.* New York: Pantheon, 1992.

Moyers, Bill.   "A Conversation with Toni Morrison." *A World of Ideas II,* edited by Andie Tucher. Garden City: Doubleday, 1990. ●

Naylor, Gloria.   "Gloria Naylor and Toni Morrison: A Conversation." *Southern Review* 21, No. 3, July 1985. ●◆

Neustadt, Kathy.   Interview with Toni Morrison. *Bryn Mawr Alumnae Bulletin,* Spring 1980. ●

O'Brien, Edna.   Review of *Jazz. New York Times Book Review,* April 5, 1992. ■

Pagels, Elaine.   *The Gnostic Gospels.* New York: Random House, 1979.

Price, Reynolds.   Review of *Song of Solomon. New York Times Book Review,* September 11, 1977. ■◆

Robinson, James M.   (General Editor). *The Nag Hammadi Library.* New York: HarperCollins, 1990. The complete Gnostic scriptures translated into English. (Referred to in chapters on *Jazz* and *Paradise.*)

Ruas, Charles.   From *Conversations with American Writers.* New York: McGraw Hill, 1984. (The two-part interview took place in 1981. To the best of my knowledge, it was not published until 1984.) ●

Rubenstein, Roberta.   *Boundaries of the Self: Gender, Culture, Fiction.* © 1987 by the board of Trustees of the University of Illinois. ■

Schappell, Elissa and Lacour, Claudia Brodsky.   "Toni Morrison: The Art of Fiction." *Paris Review,* Fall 1993.

Sissman, L.E.   Review of *The Bluest Eye. New Yorker,* January 23, 1971. ■◆

Smith, Dinitia.   Review of *Paradise. New York Times,* January 8, 1998.

Spillers, Hortense J.   "A Hateful Passion, a Lost Love" from *Feminist Studies* 9, Summer 1983. ■

Stepto, Robert.   " 'Intimate Things in Place': A Conversation with Toni Morrison." *Massachusetts Review* 18, Autumn 1977. ■●

Strouse, Jean.   "Toni Morrison's Black Magic." *Newsweek,* March 30, 1981.

Tate, Claudia. Interview with Toni Morrison. *Black Women Writers at Work,* edited by Claudia Tate. New York: Continuum, 1983. ●

Taylor-Guthrie, Danille. Introduction to *Conversations with Toni Morrison,* edited by Danille Taylor-Guthrie. Jackson: University Press of Mississippi, 1994.

Washington, Elise. "A conversation with Toni Morrison." *Essence,* October, 1987. ●

Watkins, Mel. Review of *Tar Baby. New York Times Book Review,* September 11, 1977. ●

Wilson, Judith. "A conversation with Toni Morrison." *Essence,* July 1981. ●

# INDEX